RABBINIC JUDAISM'S GENERATIVE LOGIC

RABBINIC JUDAISM'S GENERATIVE LOGIC

VOLUME ONE

THE MAKING OF THE MIND OF JUDAISM

JACOB NEUSNER

Academic Studies in the History of Judaism
Global Publications, Binghamton University
Binghamton, New York
2002

Copyright © 2002 by Jacob Neusner

Cover artwork by Suzanne R. Neusner.

Library of Congress Cataloging-in-Publication Data

Neusner, Jacob, 1932-
  Rabbinic Judaism's generative logic / Jacob Neusner.
      v. cm. -- (Academic studies in the history of Judaism)
  Includes bibliographical references.
  Contents: v. 1. The making of the mind of Judaism -- v. 2. The formation of the Jewish intellect, making connections and drawing conclusions in the traditional system of Judaism.
   ISBN 1-58684-181-5 (v. 1) -- ISBN 1-58684-182-3 (v. 2)
   1. Rabbinical literature--History and criticism--Theory, etc. 2. Judaism--Essence, genius, nature. 3. Judaism--History--Talmudic period, 10-425. 4. Tradition (Judaism)--History. I. Title. II. Series.
   BM496.5 .N48173 2002
   296.1'206'01--dc21
                                                                2002001672

Published and distributed by:
Academic Studies in the History of Judaism
Global Publications, Binghamton University
State University of New York at Binghamton
LNG 99, Binghamton University
Binghamton, New York, USA 13902-6000
Phone: (607) 777-4495. Fax: 777-6132
E-mail: pmorewed@binghamton.edu
http://ssips.binghamton.edu and
http://globalpublicationspress.com

ACADEMIC STUDIES
IN THE HISTORY OF JUDAISM

Publisher: Global Publications, State University of New York at Binghamton
Address: LNG 99, SUNY-Binghamton, Binghamton, New York, 13902-6000

TABLE OF CONTENTS

VOLUME ONE

THE MAKING OF THE MIND OF JUDAISM

PREFACE

By "mind" or thought. I mean, specifically, the logic that generates new truth out of established fact. That generative logic dictates, first, how people connect one thing to something else, one fact to another, in literary terms, one sentence to another; and, second, the ways they form connections into large-scale conclusions, encompassing statements. Generative logic then determines how the result of connection generates large-scale construction of ideas. These two stages — the perception of connection between two things, the discernment of (self-evidently valid) conclusions based on the connection — characterize the normative mind of a culture. They further allow us to explore the potentialities and also the limitations of intellect, what people are likely to see or to miss. In these two volumes I explain how the authoritative, canonical documents of Rabbinic Judaism in its formative age signal the generative logic that animates all thought that is embodied in those writings.

This project treats as a continuous account of, and condenses two monographs on, the foundations of self-evidence in Rabbinic Judaism as represented by its formative canon, from the Mishnah through the Bavli. The two are as follows:

- *The Making of the Mind of Judaism.* Atlanta, 1987: Scholars Press for Brown Judaic Studies.
- *The Formation of the Jewish Intellect. Making Connections and Drawing Conclusions in the Traditional System of Judaism.* Atlanta, 1988: Scholars Press for Brown Judaic Studies.

The studies were connected, the second carrying forward the problem of the first, and they were meant to be read together and in sequence. There is a measure of overlap and some repetition, which I have tried to keep to a minimum. I omitted a chapter of the original *Formation* as well as a fair amount of illustrative material. But the two parts, while connected, do not repeat the main points. For first asks, in the context of the modes of constructive, coherent thought of the canonical writings, why no science in Judaism, such as the Mishnah could have sustained. For its part the second compares and contrasts the means of making connections and drawing conclusions of Judaism and Christianity, respectively: the one through the medium of the Talmud of Babylonia, the other through the medium of Scripture, thus, the Bavli versus the Bible.

The problem I address in asking about the generative logic of Rabbinic Judaism is simple: what are the rules of cogency, of coherent discourse, that everybody in the normative documents for granted, that is, what defines the self-evidence of the intellectual system of that Judaism? The Foreword of the first of the two parts of this project specifies what is at stake here: the intellectual basis on which the paramount Judaism of the ages engages, or does not engage, with the modern and contemporary sciences, democracy, capitalism, and philosophy. The Foreword of the second explains the comparison of the generative logics of several Judaisms, the Pentateuch, the system animating the Qumran Library, the Mishnah, the Talmud, and the Bible (that is, encompassing, as heir of Scripture, Christianity in the Bible).

I express my thanks to Professor David Ruderman, University of Pennsylvania, for his valuable reflections, in his work on science in Judaism, on the original publication of *Making of the Mind* and this re-presentation of it in its larger monographic context.

I am further grateful to Global Publications for its publication of monographs of mine. Dr. Parviz Morewedge is a model of the academic entrepreneur, who makes possible the work of scholarship and its dissemination.

Jacob Neusner

Research Professor of Religion and Theology
Bard College
Annandale-on-Hudson, New York 12504
Neusner@webjogger.net

FOREWORD TO
THE MAKING OF THE MIND OF JUDAISM

The three definitive components of Western civilization, in politics, economics, and philosophy (modes of intellect), have precipitated for the Judaism of the dual Torah, in Europe and America, a chronic crisis. Minds educated in that Judaism and through sustained exegetical study of its principal documents have coped only with difficulty with democracy, capitalism, and science (including technology). Exegetical inquiry into the meanings of words and phrases, at which the faithful prove adept, do not sustain large-scale experimental thought. Exegesis without hermeneutics does not support hermeneutics.

Whatever the role of individual Jews, generally secular for generations, minds educated solely in the schools and holy books of the Judaism of the dual Torah — its institutions and formative intellect — have made no contribution to the framing of these definitive forces of modern life and thought. Science, politics, economics, and philosophy, have emerged elsewhere than from within the mind and imagination of thinkers nurtured solely by the canonical writings of that Judaism. While Jews sustained by a different Judaism, or by no Judaism at all, found in democracy, capitalism, and science and technology, politics, philosophy, and economics the sources for right thinking and worthwhile living, the institutions and intellect of the Judaism of the dual Torah have not.

Part of the reason is political, sociological, and institutional, the hierarchism and authoritarianism of the schools and the documents that contain their lessons. In the Judaism of the dual Torah, decision-making, individual and institutional, referred to the authority of sages. Sustained, systematic, rational economic activity took a subordinate place, well behind study of the Torah, as the paramount activity of men's lives (but not women's). Scientific learning, sustained experiment in the testing of propositions, systematic skepticism concerning received truths were held as matters of triviality, wasting time best spent in Torah-study, which, to be sure, had its canons of the testing of proposition and its disciplines of systematic skepticism. Only integrationist Orthodox-Judaism, which taught not only Talmud but technology and science in its schools and universities, forms an exception to this rule, but it is the exception that proves the point. Only by setting aside valuable time and energy from Torah-study to the study of science, philosophy, and social science have Yeshiva University and Bar Ilan University found their place in contemporary learning. Their segregationist-counterparts within the Torah-camp have not attempted to do so, and do not possess the intellectual resources to try. Here I show that the reason is not doctrinal. It derives from the very fundamental modes of thought and inquiry inculcated by the holy books, thus, "why no science?"

In the State of Israel today, the dominant sector of the Judaism of the dual Torah, in its institutions and attitudes, carries forward the quite different ideals of politics, economic action, and intellectual life that that Judaism maintains were received from Sinai (as the system would say). When we consider the Protestant Christian sources of democracy and (it is commonly maintained) also of capitalism, and the Christian Orthodox, Protestant, and Roman Catholic origins of science among the faithful of the Church for long centuries prior to the outbreak of the war between religion and science, we recognize through the comparison and contrast that a question of considerable interest awaits attention: why there, not here? This book therefore proposes to explain why the normative modes of thought and intellect, which I call, "the mind," of the Judaism of the dual Torah did not generate the kind of thinking that produced science, the division of philosophy known until nearly our own day as natural philosophy.

I shall specify the paramount processes of thought as they emerged in concrete writings of the age and show how each comes to full and rich realization in some of those writings. Then I shall point to two particular modes of thought as paramount, one in the composition of propositions, the other in the joining of propositions into large-scale and sustained discourses. At the end I shall ask the speculative question, of why minds educated and also wholly retained by the modes of thought of this Judaism did not produce science as we know it in the West. For that seems to me the single most interesting and even urgent question we in the age of science and technology can address to any system of intellect, that is, manner of mind educated to make connections and draw conclusions in one way, rather than in some (any) other. Anyone interested in the description, analysis, and interpretation of the cultural life of any social group will want to know the answer to three questions: did this culture generate democracy, capitalism, and science, if so, why, if not, why not? For we shall understand the world we know only when we grasp the choices humanity has faced, the decisions, articulated or merely implicit, we make in creating the world as we do rather than in some other way. Since, as is clear, we in the West have made choices of a political, economic, and intellectual system different from the choices made elsewhere in times past and in our own day, we owe to ourselves a clear explanation of what we do in comparison to what others have done and now do. In responding to that question, Judaism, particularly the Judaism of the dual Torah, promises important answers, indeed, answers disproportionately influential to the small numbers of people who adhere to that Judaism.

The order of argument is simple. In Chapter One I set forth the question and the context in which evidence I shall adduce in answering it took shape. In Chapter Two I show that distinctive modes of thought produced a kind of writing in Judaism quite different in the basic structure of its mentality and interior traits of logic and, especially, the formation of large-scale structures of knowledge, from the kind of writing carried out by contemporary Christian theologians — even on the same questions. I then, in Chapters Three through Six, describe and analyze, in the context of the concrete expression of mind provided by principal canonical writings, the four critical processes of thought, which I call logics, as I see them, three propositional logics, the philosophical, teleological, and metaproposition, and one non-propositional logic, the logic of fixed association.

In Chapter Seven I answer the question at hand: why this, not that: why no science in Judaism? My answer appeals to modes of thought in particular. I point to the particular logics that prevailed and so, for fifteen hundred years, defined the mind of Judaism. I lay out the way in which Jews within the Judaic system of the dual Torah, first, would deem self-evident the connections between one thing and something else, second, would deem natural the manner of drawing conclusions from those connections, and, third, would regard as given the range of issues to be addressed. I explain how and why that two of the four logics predominated, even while all four logics served, and then show the incongruity between that mixed logic of medium and large-scale discourse and the fundamental logic of philosophy, including natural philosophy. In that way I shall offer my explanation of why the mind of Judaism did not think philosophically-scientifically. So in that chapter I claim to account for why those few Jews in medieval times who philosophized trained their minds to think in a way different from the received one, and why those many Jews in modern times who did become scientists found they had to leave the institutions of the Judaism of the dual Torah if they were brought up in them and in all cases educated themselves in modes of thought different from (among the still-pious, in addition to) the Judaic ones.

My fundamental argument is that the paramount documents of Judaism not only preserved, but also inculcated, a particular way of forming propositions, which, in this book, I refer to as putting two and two together to equal four — the italicized words forming the hinge on which all else turns — and also a particular mode of joining these propositions together into sizable compositions of thought. The very means by which these modes of thought were transmitted and held together, the extraordinary power of analysis and argument characteristic of the normative documents — these explain also the incapacity of those same modes of thought to frame philosophy, including natural philosophy. The power is the pathos of the system. And in the end I shall account for the difficulty that the Judaism of the dual Torah confronted in focusing upon issues of natural philosophy or science in particular. By the making of the mind of Judaism, therefore, I mean the modes of thought characteristic of the normative statements of a particular Judaism.

II

When I speak of "the making of the mind of Judaism," I refer, specifically, to the setting forth of those processes of thought that taught people to see things in one way and not in some other and to say things in this way, not in that way. An on-going social entity inculcates in age succeeding age modes of thought that, shared by all, impart self-evidence and enduring sense to transient propositions. Minds may change on this and that. But mind does not, mind meaning modes of patterned thought on ephemera. Accordingly, while the social entity undergoes change, rules of deliberation dictate the range of permissible deed, and the realm of choice honors limits set by sense deemed common. How people think dictates the frontiers of possibility. The mind of Judaism, that is to say, process, is what will define Judaism in age succeeding age, so long as a Judaic system endures.

For "mind" in this project, both here and in the companion volume, I use a simple word, logic, to stand for this principle of intelligibility and cogency of thought and the expression of thought in public discourse. Logic is what joins one sentence to the next and forms the whole into paragraphs of meaning, intelligible propositions, each with its place and sense in a still larger, accessible system. Because of logic one mind connects to another, public discourse becomes possible, debate on issues of general intelligibility takes place, and an anthology of statements about a single subject becomes a composition of theorems about that subject. What people think — exegesis in accord with a fixed hermeneutic of the intellect — knows no limit. How they think makes all the difference.

When we can describe the mind of a social entity through sorting out the rules governing the reaching of discrete and disparate conclusions, then we can claim to understand how the mind of a society of like-minded people is formed, those generative rules of culture and regulations of intellect that succeeding generations receive from infancy and transmit to an unknowable future. Attitudes shift. Values and beliefs change. One generation's immutable truths come to the coming age as banalities or nonsense. But processes of reflection about the sense of things, modes of thought concerning how we identify and solve problems, above all, the making of connections between this and that — these endure like oceans and mountains. Shifting only in tides and currents so vast as to defy the grasp of time, so that, when they do quake, the whole earth moves, these processes and modes of mind in the end dictate structure and establish order, the foundations of all social life, the framework of all culture.

Here I tell the story of how a well-composed and powerfully framed mode of deliberation, a manner of seeing things in one way rather than in some other, took shape in the formative age of the Judaism of the dual Torah that has constituted Judaism from the seventh century to our own time. That manner of seeing things, in particular told people how to make connections between one thing and another and drew and composed in large-scale constructions the conclusions dictated by those connections, which is to say, how to make sense of detail and hold the whole together. My claim to describe, analyze, and interpret the mind of Judaism appeals to the paramount status of a single, normative and norm-defining document, to which people turned for the details of how to conduct themselves, and which, in consequence, imparted not only information, but, through recurrent acts of consultation, a mode of thought as well. That single document, the Talmud of Babylonia or Bavli, so dominated the life of Jews in both Christian and Muslim civilizations that that writing formed the academy of the mind of Judaism. Therefore when we can characterize the mind conveyed within the pages of that writing, we may accurately assess the intellect of those whose lives found structure and sense there and nowhere else.

The category "mind" invokes vast spaces. But I mean something very concrete, which we can examine and replicate in mental experiments. By "mind" I mean processes of thought that instruct people how to make connections and draw conclusions from them, the way in which to put two facts, hence two sentences, together in a cogent union and to made an intelligible statement to others. In later discussion I identify "mind" with the sentence "two *and* two *equal* four," and the italicized words, *and* and *equal,* stand in an acutely concrete and specific way for mind or intellect. By Judaism I mean the Judaism of the dual Torah, oral and written, that comes to its climactic expression in the Talmud of Babylonia. By the formative age I intend to speak of the first through the seventh centuries.

The mind of Judaism is made up by intellectuals, people who see connections and therefore draw conclusions — and frame documents, e.g., write books. They are the makers of the world, the unacknowledged legislators of all realms of human action in society. I want to know how the definitive writings of a particular Judaism derived from one way of discerning connections rather than from some other, and, furthermore, how those same writings then instructed Jews for many centuries to draw conclusions in one way, rather than in some other. For thoughtful people ask why when others find only self-evidence, and the Judaism of the dual Torah is the invention of thought. The making of the mind of Judaism took place in the first seven centuries of the Common Era (=A.D.) and reached complete realization in the canonical writings of the Judaism of the dual Torah, culminating, in the single definitive statement, in the Talmud of Babylonia or Bavli. The mind of Judaism educated in the processes of reflection and argument formed by the Bavli dictated how right-thinking people would recognize order in chaos, make sense of nonsense, see connections, draw conclusions, in all, determine the rules and regularities of reality.

We in the contemporary West readily understand what is at stake in the formation of the shared and social intellect of an entire community of mind; it is the discovery of knowledge we today call scientific or philosophical. The mind of Judaism, like Western science and the great tradition of philosophy, undertook the quest for "unity underlying apparent diversity, simplicity underling apparent complexity, order underlying apparent disorder, regularity underlying apparent anomaly." The quest for order and (therefore also) explanation required the making of connections between one thing and something else and the drawing of conclusions from those discerned connections. At issue in this book, therefore, is how the mind of Judaism, portrayed by the canonical writings of the formative age, understood the making of connections and the drawing of conclusions.

The specific question I answer therefore is a very simple one of how the mind of Judaism sees the connections between one thing and something else and draws conclusions from the connections that are discerned. Stated in more general terms, my proposition is that an explanation of mind matters because it tells us how an intellect common to a number of authoritative writings — hence, to a textual community — altogether makes sense of things. Modes of thought transform information into knowledge, identify questions and answer them. People who think in a shared way communicate and so form a community of sense, able to transact exchanges and accomplish shared discourse. Here I describe the interior cogency of the writings of people who form a textual community, that is, whose writings all together are received as a single seamless statement of truth and for centuries continue to dictate not only truth but how truth may be known and tested. Modes of thought common to a social, entity of one type or another characterize that group and dictate some of its indicative traits. The community of Judaism constitutes one such social entity, which from the seventh through the nineteenth century appealed to a single document not only for information but also for correct rules about gaining information. Here I define what I conceive to be those rules.

The fundamental premise of this book, on which all else rests, is simple. It is that intellect endures in language, modes of thought in syntax and sentence structure, which realize in concrete ways abstract processes of reasoning. The mind of Judaism reaches us only in its results, the sentences formed into paragraphs, the paragraphs into chapters, the chapters into books: the truths deemed self-evidently valid, the propositions held beyond all debate, yielding the intense disagreement on this and that that serves as the wherewithal of everyday thought. The stakes in writing are higher still. For the books of a long-dead past live on and shape the everyday reality of Judaism today. The mind of Judaism exists in the here and now of decisions on what I should do and why I should do it, the meaning of things, the past and future, the hope and destination, the sense of the whole and the fittingness of each part. The stakes are very high.

If. Therefore. we wish to understand what people think, we had best first ask how they think, and to know how people think, we analyze their writing: modes of making up sentences and joining them together into paragraphs, manner of composing paragraphs into chapters, chapters into books — all translated into the abstractions of knowledge, from fact to proposition, from proposition to encompassing theory. That means explaining the ways in which they choose the problems they find urgent, know that one set of data pertains and another does not. So we have to account for how the writers of authoritative documents make connections between this and that. All of these abstracts come to immediate and concrete expression not in sentences but in paragraphs, that is to say, in the composition of two or more sentences. These points of union, the joining of two facts into a proposition that transcends them both, the making of a whole that exceeds the sum of the parts — these acts of intellectual enchantment wonderfully form the smallest whole units of propositional thought. When, therefore, we know why this, not that, why a paragraph looks one way, rather than some other, we find ourselves at the very center xxiv

Jacob Neusner

of the working of a mind: its making of sense out of the nonsense presented by the detritus of mere information.

What is not at stake in this book is sociology or cultural anthropology. I claim to describe and account for the shape and structure of intellect of a socially-facing system of intellect, a Judaism, that alone, and not Jews' culture. I do not claim that all, or most, or at least all "authentic," Jews think, characteristically, in one way and not in some other. If made as a statement of either negative evaluation or self-praise (e.g., why do, or did, Jews win so many Nobel prizes in sciences?), it would form an expression of mere racism or ethnic aggrandizement, therefore one of no-account romanticism. If made as an allegation of fact, that would constitute a statement of sociology or of cultural anthropology, not one of the logic of connection, such as I wish to make. Pertinent evidence for those fields derives not only from the and that joins sentences or the equal that forms of sentences a syllogism. Other facts intervene.

More to the point, I know no studies that demonstrate for us the claim that there is a distinctively "Jewish" way of thought, characteristic of all Jews and no gentiles. But there was, and is, a religious system, a Judaism, with its own rules of intellect and conduct, its integrity, its definitive (and therefore, to itself) unique traits. And in the canonical writings of that Judaism I can show that there was, and is, a distinctively (but none can claim, uniquely) Judaic mode of thought. For, as I shall demonstrate, as a matter of description of the logic of connection, the canonical writings of Judaism do reach and express conclusions in one way and not in some other, and I therefore can provide an account of the making of the mind of not the Jews but Judaism: the canonical writings, seen whole and complete, that constitute the statement of Judaism, its world-view, way of life, and address to the social entity, "Israel," of its invention.

I stress that I of course do not allege that the principal repertoire of logics characteristic of the canonical authorships is distinctive to that canon, for that is something I cannot show and therefore do not know. I suspect that we may point to other religious systems that appeal for cogency and order to those same principles that operate in

Judaism. I have the impression that the peculiar mode of dialectical argument to which I appeal in the end is uncommon in modes of thought overall. But I allege only that people who form the authorships of canonical writings did make choices and did determine in one way and not in some other to form their cogent statements of connection, to draw conclusion from discerned connection. What is characteristic of a group of writings tells us how those writers thought, and I claim to describe that mode of thought without alleging no other group of writers thought that way, let alone that all writers within Judaism from then to now thought that way and no other way. Describing traits characteristic of one set of writings requires, as I shall explain, showing that people made choices, not that their choices were unique to them.

Still, as a matter of fact, I tend to think that the Bavli forms an instrument of cultural expression and continuity without significant parallel in the history of the literate cultures of humanity — though each, self-evidently, has had its equivalent to the Bavli. But comparisons of a global nature lie far beyond the distant horizons of this exercise, even though, I do believe, the time will come, also, for comparison, even of considerable dimensions indeed. And, as I said at the outset, the two other formative and definitive traits of the world we know, capitalism and democracy, also emerged within religious worlds other than the Judaic one, and that too requires explanation. But not here, not now, and not necessarily by me. Now to the task at hand.

CHAPTER ONE

THE MAKING OF THE MIND OF JUDAISM

Like any other great mode of construction of society and intellect, whether the tradition of Western philosophy from Greece, or the great edifice of Christianity, the Confucian tradition in China, or science and technology of our own age, the Judaism of the dual Torah, — in its way of life, world view, and identification of the social entity, the "Israel," to which it speaks, — comprises monumental answers to fundamental questions framed and answered by thoughtful people. Identifying critical questions and responding with self-evidently valid answers, intellectuals laid down the boundaries of an ordered world. Now when we know not only the questions and the answers, but also the modes of thought that made the former urgent and the latter self-evidently true, we penetrate into the heart of the matter of ordering the social world: the processes of making connections and reaching conclusions that, in the end, produced the questions and the answers that, all together, ultimately constituted Judaism. God — so to speak — spoke not only in presence but also in proposition. The Judaism of the dual Torah attests to not only the public event of the Torah but also to the processes that (as a matter of fact) yielded, also, the Torah.

Let me now reframe the program of this book in more concrete and less mythic terms. If we want to understand how the intellectuals of a social entity make sense of things, we examine the language they use in order to speak sensibly. That language presents the evidence on how people both reach and convey conclusions of consequence. When we can understand how people discern relationship between one fact, that is, one sentence, and another fact or sentence and further set forth conclusions to be drawn from the relationship or connection, we know not only what they think, but, from the character of the connection, how they think. So God lives in the syntax of cogent thought and intelligible statement of thought, and Judaism is the statement of process, yielding, of course, proposition as well. The propositions vary from document to document (though of course cogent all together), but the process, which characterizes all documents, uniformly imposes its connections and ubiquitously generates its conclusions. That matter of process grasped, we know how the mind of that social entity frames the propositions that it proposes as its system and the foundation of its order. Accordingly, by definition the logic of intelligible discourse, the premise of self-evident comprehension, above all, the intangible sensibility that makes connections between one thing and something else and yields conclusions transcending them both — these are what hold together many minds in one community of shared and mutually intelligible speech that, in the aggregate, we may call society, in our instance, the society of Judaism or the "Israel" at hand. The evidence for that shared intellect, that mind in common, therefore comes to us in how people speak to one another, in the connections each makes between two or more sentences and in the connections all make with one another. The formation of a shared intellect, the making of a mind in common — these derive from process and connection. This book aims to describe the making of the mind of Judaism, by which I mean, the ways in which authorships of the formative canonical writings of Judaism defined connections between one sentence and another and drew conclusions from those connections, the public logic of common and (perceivedly) cogent discourse.

When we can trace, through the writings of a given social entity, the unfolding of modes of thought, identifying the choices afforded to intellectuals by those received modes of thought, we may fairly claim to know how a social entity, in its enduring cultural heritage, has made up its mind — and of what that mind consists in its fundamental structure. That social entity, in the case of the authorships of the documents deemed canonical by the Judaism that took shape between the first and the seventh centuries, called the Judaism of the dual Torah, comprises a textual community. By that I mean, the authorships that, all together, stand behind writings deemed to form not merely a compilation or a library of writings, but a coherent canon of authoritative law and theology. That textual community is amply documented by the canonical writings of the Judaism of the dual Torah. Its writings, then, carry us deep within its processes of thought, the ways in which it makes connections between one thing and another and makes of the two something new again. That textual community made up the mind of Judaism, and its principal writings for close to two millennia then educated Jews' minds. So long as the paramount authority of the canon governed Israel's intellect, as it did from the seventh through the nineteenth centuries, the mind of Judaism dictated the traits of intellect of the minds of Jews. At stake, therefore, in inquiring into the formation of the mind of Judaism is the framing of that world of private thought and public conscience, individual intellect and public sensibility, that Jews comprised.

When Jews, including Judaists deeply learned in the Judaism of the dual Torah, worked out their intellectual lives solely within the intellect of that Judaism, they did not create philosophy or science, which, for those Judaists within the received intellectual disciplines, required modes of thought quite different in large-scale composition from the ones taught by those received disciplines. By science I mean two things. First comes the counterpart, in English, of the word Wissenschaft in German, that is to say, I refer first of all to philosophy as systematic, critical, orderly entertaining and testing of encompassing propositions meant to identify and account for rules and regularities among things: connections and propositions explaining them. In that sense, I have in mind something akin to philosophy in its deepest sense: knowledge acquired in an orderly manner and composed in a critical spirit — and also presented in a systematic, orderly way, along lines dictated by its intrinsic program and characteristics. Not only the creation of knowledge but its formation in systematic constructions defines the issue. But I use the word science in its second, American sense: natural science and social science, a very particular component of philosophy, which, before the last century, were called natural philosophy and social philosophy.

The Judaism of the dual Torah within its own modes of intellect produced little philosophy, both in general and also in the particular natural and social forms that flourished in Christianity and Islam in the same time and circumstance. Where philosophy made its way within Jewry, its modes of thought were perceived as alien and necessitated sustained labors of harmonization. Where for whatever reasons philosophy found no hearing among the intellectuals of the Judaism of the dual Torah, there was no philosophy, nor any science, produced among those intellectuals. Everyone knows the story of the rich philosophical tradition precipitated by the Muslim mediation of the philosophical tradition of antiquity to both Judaism and Christianity. But where philosophy did not enter from without, it also did not germinate from within.

That claim of mine is captured by the simple fact that Copernicus was a monk in Roman Catholic Poland in the sixteenth century and that the Church for purposes of accurately calculating the calendar assigned him the task that he performed, with unanticipated results to be sure. In Judaic Poland in that same century flourished countless towering intellectual figures within the Judaism of the dual Torah; whatever bits and pieces of scientific, including medical knowledge any of them possessed, none of them known to us pursued questions of a scientific character in a philosophical manner, in the way in which their countryman and contemporary, Copernicus, did. Neither the methods nor the subject-matter of science enjoyed systematic entry in the institutions of the dual Torah in Poland of that period, any more than in the contemporary institutions of the same Judaism, in the State of Israel and the USA, for example, science and technology form part of the curriculum of learning. And, of course, Copernicus stood in a long line of tradition, extending backward to the origins of Christian philosophy in Greece and forward into the seventeenth century.

Nor did the Christian impetus for science end there within the scientific traditions of the Roman Catholic Church, medieval or early modern; Mendelev, founder of genetics, we recall, was an Orthodox Christian monk. And the role of Protestant Christian philosophers, including scientists, in both the Reformation Churches and the free churches, hardly requires a sizable repertoire of instances. I may therefore stipulate as fact that until the seventeenth century science, as a division of philosophy, formed an important component of the intellectual life of the principal systems of Christianity, east and west, Greek and Latin. By science in the topical context I mean interest in physics, chemistry, biology, botany, and the other standard fields and disciplines as well; and also social science and other subdivisions of social and political and even economic philosophy. I do not refer in particular to those traits of mind of science, such as skepticism and resort to experiment and the amassing of data, that have come to characterize science in the more recent centuries; these traits became normative in those centuries in which Christianity and science parted company and lie beyond the argument of this book. I maintain that the Judaism of the dual Torah did not yield science, while, in the same times and circumstances, diverse Christian systems did. And I want to know what characterized the mind of Judaism that made philosophy, including natural philosophy, an uncommon outcome of intellectual inquiry: why this, not that?

The mind of Judaism comprises those processes of thought that tell people why one thing is self-evidently connected with some other and that furthermore instruct them how to draw conclusions from the connection. The modes of thought paramount in the canonical writings of the Judaism of the dual Torah in its formative age are what I propose to describe, analyze, and interpret. The reason I think I can do so is that we have in those canonical writings of Judaism, from the first through the seventh century, ample evidence of the results of how people have thought deeply and abstractly, the concrete evidences, in language, of the conduct of thought. From the language people used to say what they were thinking, I propose to move backward to the processes of thought encapsulated in that language. If people state a proposition, I want to know the argumentation in behalf of that proposition, the kind of evidence and the manner of marshalling that evidence. Still more to the point, if people see a connection, I want to ask what makes the connection self-evident to them, so that one thing fits with some other, and another thing does not. For the mind of Judaism is not abstract , and the Judaism that that mind defines does not deal solely in abstractions. The authors of the canonical writings of the Judaism of the formative age mastered the requirements of applied reason and practical logic. But that means they also were masters of intellect and logical acumen. Consequently, we have in hand ample evidence, in concrete terms, of both the decisions people reached and the ways in which they framed their propositions. That is why I claim the mind of Judaism finds ample documentation in the writings of Judaism. And — so I maintain — we may reconstruct how people think from what they say. And because, for long centuries, all Judaists read the same books and communicated within the patterns of thought inculcated by those books, we may speak not only of the mind of Judaism but also the textual community that embodied and realized that mind.

The bridge from proposition, that is, what people think, to process, how they think, therefore is built of modes of discourse preserved and transmitted in writing: mutually intelligible exchanges of ideas, in fully articulated language made up of words and sentences that follow a public syntax. Discourse thus refers to the way in which people make their statements so that the connections within their thought are intelligible and cogent to others (and that by definition, hence the stress on the public). To describe the modes of discourse which attest to modes of thought at the deep structure of mind, we ask how people place on display not only the conclusions they have reached but also the manner in which they wish to announce and argue in favor of those conclusions — all together, the way in which they make their statement of their position. Accordingly, it is in cogent argument concerning proposition that mind becomes incarnate.

That is why in this book I work my way back from the way in which people compose their cogent and persuasive statements to the mind, the intellect, that teaches them not only or mainly what to think, but rather, how to think. My claim is that the intellect, an abstraction, finds form in a fully-exposed manner of reaching and demonstrating a particular statement of sense. In the canonical writings of the Judaism studied here — the Judaism of the dual Torah that has constituted normative Judaism from the seventh century, the time of the closure of the Talmud of Babylonia or Bavli, to the present day — the intellect of Judaism finds realization. That intellect or mind takes place, for instance, in the framing of a proposition, complete in exposition, from beginning statement through middle demonstration and argumentation to end conclusion and the drawing of consequences. For mind cannot endure in abstract theory, contemplating itself alone, but has its work to do. The result of that labor of thought is the Judaism of the dual Torah, expressed in the canonical writings of the first seven centuries A.D., and in this book I wish to show the making of that mind of the Judaism that those writings state.

Here therefore I propose to tell the story of the formation of the mind of Judaism, accounting in terms of how authorships composed their actual writings for how the Judaism presented by a particular set of canonical writings reached the conclusions that it did. It is a story, but the story is not guided by chronology. This is not a history of the intellect of Judaism, because I do not claim that there was a "traditional" or received mode of thought, which gave way to a "new" or different one. Sequence describes, it does not explain, and the sequential order of things does not lead us into the depths of logic and of structure. My story narrates not the history of literature, first this book, then that book, but rather the tale of thought: the account of the stages of mindful analysis of how people reached conclusions.

I propose to explain how authorships both made connections between one thing and something else and drew conclusions from those connections. For that purpose I start in the middle of things, with a document that contains within itself all four "logics" of cogent discourse that I claim define the repertoire of intellect of Judaism, that modes of making connections and drawing conclusions from them. Then I proceed to survey a variety of documents, asking which logic of connection and conclusion — the discovery of order and rule — predominates in each. At the end I point to the Bavli as the definitive statement of the whole, on the one side, but also as the source of the subsequent emphasis upon a single mode of thought, on the other.

That is why I propose to tell the story, through an account of the logics of intelligible discourse and their use, of how the mind of Judaism — the Judaism of the dual Torah, written and oral, that has dictated the norms and determined the structure of most Jewries in the world until nearly our own day — was formed. For, as a matter of fact, Jewries in both Christian and Muslim worlds appealed to a single document for the law and theology that shaped their common way of life and world view, and they found in that document the identification and definition of the social entity that they themselves constituted, namely, "Israel." The Judaism of the dual Torah, its world-view, way of life, and understanding of the social entity, "Israel," constituted by its devotees, reached its conclusions in perpetual conversation with a single classic writing; educated its coming generations in not only its contents but its manner of reaching conclusions; constituted, in any one location, the embodiment of its statement of the sacred. Accordingly, when we can trace the modes of thought available to the framers of that paramount and definitive documentary statement of the whole, we know what I claim to account for here, which is how the mind of Judaism was formed. The document to which I refer, of course, is the Talmud of Babylonia, or Bavli, and from that writing I look backward, over the artifacts of the textual community that reached its final and complete statement within the Bavli. I survey modes of thought (a term defined in a moment) available to the framers of the Bavli and show how each one worked. Then, at the end, I shall point to the mode of thought selected by the Bavli's framers and propose to account for why that one way of thinking proved paramount.

At stake, however, is not only or even principally the Bavli and its modes of thought. At issue is a variety of writings, held authoritative and therefore holy along with the Bavli. These form not only a collection but a canon. But the canonicity until now has been imputed, not demonstrated from within; people know that works form canonical documents, and then impute to each such writing the propositions and doctrine of all others. They view the whole as seamless and forming a single uniform statement, complete and final, wherever we turn. The lines of documents for the faithful in no way differentiate. When we ask how the result of reading the documents one by one yields the conclusions just now outlined, we of course find considerable difficulty, since documents read one by one look remarkably distinctive. I claim, within the argument before us, that what joins one document to the next to form a sustained canonical statement is not content (which may vary, for instance, in topics treated) but modes of making connections, not in propositions but in process. Once more, in our quest for the shared premises of behavior and belief, that is, for the propositions of the Judaism at hand, we direct our gaze to the less tangible data of the processes of thought, in particular those of establishing connections and generating cogent conversation. So, once more, our examination of the modes of thought will draw us inward, to the deepest levels of public discourse.

Now let me spell out the order of argument. This is an inquiry into the history not of writings but of the logic of writing, by which I mean, the joining of sentence to sentence into an intelligible statement. But that account is not historical at all. For we cannot show that people first thought and consequently wrote in one way, then in some other. Quite to the contrary, we must take for granted that any mode of intelligible discourse now attested in a given composition presented itself as a candidate for use in public communication before its actual appearance in a given canonical book, even the first among a sequence of such books. That is why my program follows lines dictated not by the sequence in which various books first attained closure but by a different consideration altogether. The same consideration explains why the present exercise finds so slender use for history, in the same of the claim commonly made in the name of history that first came one thing, then came some other, so that the order, first this, then that, explains also the reason for the order: this generated that. I propose, instead, to follow the path of phenomenology, which is to say, to survey the possibilities yielded by the selected corpus of writings, not in their supposed order of initial appearance, but in their classifications as yielded by their final and complete canonical structure. Accordingly, I see the canonical writings as a whole and ask of them all a simple questions: how do you form sentences into paragraphs, that is to say, two or more facts into a clear proposition? how do you account for the cogency of your several self-evidently composed units of discourse (again, sentences into paragraphs), so that two or more facts, presented together, belong together?

That is why my program of exposition leads me to set forth a classification (a taxonomy) of those logics of intelligible discourse, both the ones that so work as to generate and even demonstrate propositions and those that form cogent sentences but no proposition whatsoever. Then I explain how, within the limited repertoire of logics of intelligible discourse, various canonical writings find their appropriate location. To state the main methodological plan at the outset, therefore, my interest is not in history of thought but in its phenomenology, not in the (alleged) order by which one or another mode of thought made its documentary appearance, but in the classification and definition of the types of logic at work in the making of the mind of Judaism. For I conceive the mind of Judaism to be made up by the modes of thought — hence the available logics — that yield particular propositions and make possible the statement of them. When we know the mind of a set of authorships, we should be able to explain why this, not that, meaning, how they have come to one conclusion and not to some other. And the "how" demands analysis in terms not of the conclusion reached but of the way in which reasoning works, connections are made, minds spin out their gossamer threads into webs of meaning.

We begin, however, not with my hypothesis of the logics available to our authorships but with the claim that logic matters. That is to say, I commence with evidence that the textual community whose work we survey did, indeed, think in one way and not in some other. How show that fact? Very simply, by demonstrating that there were other ways of writing — and therefore, of thinking. If I can demonstrate that people could say the same thing for different reasons and in different ways, resorting each to its own distinctive logic for the making of a statement that, in the matter of the proposition, the other party will have comprehended and wished to say for itself, then I can fairly claim that there were indeed different logics of intelligible discourse, in consequence of which the use of one, and not some other, tells us more than merely how people happened to say things. For that purpose, I contrast how two distinct worlds addressed a common issue, showing that one world made sense (for itself) in one way, another in a different way. That permits me to contend that people did make choices in how they would express their thought, and, it must follow, as we move from words to word and statements of sense to the logic that imparts self-evidence to the truth of sense, conduct their thought as well. In Chapter Two I then define what I mean by modes of thought, and in Chapter Three and the successive chapters thereafter show how these modes of thought came to expression. But at stake in this exercise is not merely a survey of the repertoire of logics and how they do their work. There is a more substantial question, for the history of Judaism, that draws me to this work of formal analysis of mind.

It may be stated very simply: is there a Judaism beyond the Judaisms of the several writings? I mean to say, can we define common to all documents of the canon? Are there indicative traits that permit us to see a basis for imputing to diverse writings the status of canonicity within the "one whole Torah of Moses, our rabbi, both written and oral," that, in secular terms, we call the Judaism of the dual Torah? We may readily show that one document intersects with some other, but we may also demonstrate that each document possesses traits of rhetoric or topic distinctive to itself. Accordingly, we wonder where we shall find that "Judaism," which is to say, that indicative and governing trait, that permits us to account for the clear and correct perception of all observers and all participants alike that there really was, and is, a Judaism, that is, a canon and not only a library. It is in the deepest layers of logical discourse, of the making of connections and consequent drawing of conclusions, that I find that -ism of the Judaism, that indicative and unifying trait of ultimate cogency that makes of the parts a single and coherent whole. It is in that same mode of thought that I find the academy for Jews, not only for Judaism, over the centuries: the school that for all educated persons defined the governing traits of mind characteristic (so many claim, I have not done the survey) of Jews' cultures as a whole, or, indeed, even of the culture formed of and by Judaism. I claim that we may define what diverse writings have in common principally by addressing a limited repertoire of processes of thought, rather than the propositional results of thought. For I contend that what characterizes in common the various writings that, all together, find a place in the canon of the Judaism subject to our study is not so much articulated proposition as premise. And the premise shared throughout concerns not so much the ways of reasoning or reaching conclusions as a much more fundamental matter, which is, the ways of making connections that sometimes yield conclusions subjected to reasoned argument and sometimes yield other intellectual statements altogether. That, then, is the story I propose to tell: how the paramount Judaism of the histories of Judaisms took shape at its most profound level, which is, the deep structure of its intellect, the making of its mind.

Now let me take up two necessary tasks of definition. First, I have briefly to define the Judaism and trace the sequence of the documents that provide our evidence for that Judaism and its mind. Second, I have to specify the class of persons to whom I impute the collective intellect or "mind" of which I speak when I talk of the making of the mind of Judaism. I refer to that category, "authorship," that implicitly predominates throughout this book. I have to justify my appeal to a collective intellect, portrayed by a given writing or document.

By "Judaism" I mean a particular Judaic system, namely, the Judaism of the dual Torah, oral and written, which in its writings and symbolic system from late antiquity to the present day has served as the paramount and definitive Judaic religious system. We know about the formative history of the Judaism of the dual Torah, oral and written, through the writings produced by sages, or rabbis, of late antiquity in the Land of Israel ("Palestine") and Babylonia, mainly the former location. Those writings fall into two groups, each with its own plan and program, the one produced in the second and third centuries, the second in the fourth and fifth. The logic revealed in these writings defines the mind of Judaism as I propose to describe that mind in its formative age.

The first of these groups of writings begins with the Mishnah, a philosophical law book brought to closure at ca. A.D. 200, later on called the first statement of the oral Torah. In its wake, the Mishnah drew tractate Abot, ca. A.D. 250, a statement of concluded a generation after the Mishnah on the standing of the authorities of the Mishnah; Tosefta, ca. A.D. 300, a compilation of supplements of various kinds to the statements in the Mishnah; and three systematic exegeses of books of Scripture or the written Torah, Sifra, to Leviticus, Sifré to Numbers, and another Sifré, to Deuteronomy, of indeterminate date but possibly concluded by A.D. 300. These books overall form one stage in the unfolding of the Judaism of the dual Torah, in which emphasis stressed issues of sanctification of the life of Israel, the people, in the aftermath of the destruction of the Temple of Jerusalem in A.D. 70, in which, it was commonly held, Israel's sanctification came to full realization in the bloody rites of sacrifice to God on high. I call this system a Judaism without Christianity, because the issues found urgent in the documents representative of this phase address questions not pertinent to the Christian défi of Israel at all. But, as to describing the regnant logic, the order of the closure of documents in succession plays no role whatsoever..

The second set of the same writings begins with the Talmud of the Land of Israel, or Yerushalmi, generally supposed to have come to a conclusion at ca. A.D. 400, Genesis Rabbah, assigned to about the next half century, Leviticus Rabbah, ca. A.D. 450, Pesiqta deRab Kahana, ca. A.D. 450-500, and, finally, the Talmud of Babylonia or Bavli, assigned to the late sixth or early seventh century, ca. A.D. 600. The two Talmuds systematically interpret passages of the Mishnah, and the other documents, as is clear, do the same for books of the written Torah. Some other treatments of biblical books important in synagogue liturgy, particularly the Five Scrolls, e.g., Lamentations Rabbati, Esther Rabbah, and the like, are supposed also to have reached closure at this time. This second set of writings introduces, alongside the paramount issue of Israel's sanctification, the matter of Israel's salvation, with doctrines of history, on the one side, and the Messiah, on the other, given prominence in the larger systemic statement.

A brief word on the history of the Judaism at hand suffices. Let me narrate that history through traits of the two distinct stages in which the writings took shape. The first of the two stages in the formation of the Judaism of the dual Torah, as I said, exhibits no sign of interest in, or response to, the advent of Christianity. The second, from the Yerushalmi forward, lays points of stress and emphasis that, in retrospect, appear to respond to, and to counter, the challenge of Christianity. The point of difference, of course, is that from the beginning of the legalization of Christianity in the early fourth century, to the establishment of Christianity at the end of that same century, Jews in the Land of Israel found themselves facing a challenge that, prior to Constantine, they had found no compelling reason to consider. The specific crisis came when the Christians pointed to the success of the Church in the politics of the Roman state as evidence that Jesus Christ was king of the world, and that his claim to be Messiah and King of Israel had now found vindication. When the Emperor Julian, 361-3, apostatized and renewed state patronage of paganism, he permitted the Jews to begin to rebuild the Temple, part of his large plan of humiliating Christianity. His prompt death on an Iranian battlefield supplied further evidence for heaven's choice of the Church and the truth of the Church's allegations concerning the standing and authority of Jesus as the Christ. The Judaic documents that reached closure in the century after these events attended to those questions of salvation, e.g., doctrine of history and of the Messiah, authority of the sages' reading of Scripture as against the Christians' interpretation, and the like, that had earlier not enjoyed extensive consideration. In all, this second Judaism, which I characterize as a Judaism despite Christianity, met the challenge of the events of the fourth century. The Judaic system of the dual Torah, expressed in its main outlines in the Yerushalmi and associated compilations of biblical exegeses concerning Genesis, Leviticus, and some other scriptural books, culminated in the Bavli, which emerged as the authoritative document of the Judaism of the dual Torah from then to now.

There are three distinct modes of organizing sustained discourse in the canon of the Judaism of the dual Torah. These cogent statements are, respectively, those built around the exegesis of the oral Torah, second, those that serve to amplify the written Torah, and, finally, those that find cogency in the life and teaching of a given sage or group of sages. To spell this out, let me explain that there were three modes of organizing large-scale discourse in the Judaism of the dual Torah. One was to make use of books or verses or themes of Scripture. A second was to follow the order of the Mishnah and compose a systematic commentary and amplification of that document. This was the way, for example, of those who created the Talmud of the Land of Israel a century or so before. A third was to organize stories about and sayings of sages. These were framed around twin biographical principles, either as strings of stories about great sages of the past or as collections of sayings and comments drawn together solely because the same name stands behind the sayings.

A tripartite corpus of inherited materials awaiting composition in a cogent composite document found its way into the Bavli. Prior to that time, the framers of documents had tended to resort to a single principle or organization, whether scriptural, Mishnaic, or biographical. The authorship of the Bavli for its part took up materials, in various states and stages of completion, pertinent to the Mishnah or to the principles of laws that the Mishnah had originally brought to articulation. Second, they had in hand received materials, again in various conditions, pertinent to the Scripture, both as the Scripture related to the Mishnah and also as the Scripture laid forth its own narratives. Finally, they collected and arranged sayings of and stories about sages. But this third principle of organizing discourse took a subordinated position, behind the other two. The framers of the Bavli organized the Bavli around the Mishnah. But, second, they adapted and included vast tracts of antecedent materials organized as scriptural commentary. These they inserted whole and complete, not at all in response to the Mishnah's program. And, finally, while making provision for compositions built upon biographical principles, preserving both strings of sayings from a given master (and often a given tradent of a given master) as well as tales about authorities of the preceding half millennium, they did nothing new. That is to say, the ultimate authorships of the canonical documents never created redactional compositions, of a sizable order, that focused upon given authorities, even though sufficient materials lay at hand to allow doing so. God's will reached Israel through Scripture, Mishnah, sage — that is, by the evidence and testimony of each of these three media equally. That is the premise of the Judaism of the entire Rabbinic canon, of each of the stories that appeal to a verse of Scripture, a phrase or sentence of the Mishnah, or a teaching or action of a sage. Recognizing the three components of the single canon, the written Torah, the oral Torah, and the sage as the living Torah, leads us deep into the investigation at hand.

    But whose mind is it that we now investigate? It is — I stress one last time — the intellect of an authorship. I call the framers of a document in the canon of the Judaism of the dual Torah "an authorship." That collectivity — one to an indeterminate number of persons, flourishing from ten minutes to five hundred years — determined and then followed fixed and public rules of orderly discourse that govern a given book's rhetoric, logic, and topic. These fixed rules, seen all together, permit us to describe the intent and program of those responsible for this writing: the authorship. Received in a canonical process of transmission under the auspices of a religious system, a Rabbinic writing enjoys authority and status within that canon and system. Hence it is deemed to speak for not a private person but a community and to represent, and contribute to, the consensus of that community. No document has a named author, for such a designation would deprive the document of all standing and authority. Accordingly, a piece of writing is represented, on the surface, as the statement of a consensus. That consensus derives not from an identifiable writer or even school but from the anonymous authorities behind the document as we have it. That is the meaning of the word "authorship," those who made up the rules of a document or later on followed them in adding to that document.

In considering any piece of writing, therefore, we have to ask whether this writing exhibits a cogent character and shows conformity to laws and regularities, therefore derives from a considered set of decisions of a rhetorical, logical, and topical order. If it does, then, as a matter of definition, it derives from an authorship, a collectivity that stands beyond the exhibited consensus in this particular writing. Accordingly, if I can find regularities of rhetoric, logic, and topical program, I claim to discern the consequences of rules people — an authorship — have made, decisions they have reached, concerning the character of this writing of theirs: its structure, organization, proposition, cogent statement. If I find no regularities and indications of an orderly program, then I may fairly claim that this writing is different from one that speaks in behalf of people who have made rules or adopted them for the inclusion of fresh ideas of their own. It belongs in a classification not of a composition but of a scrapbook, not of a collage, which uses fixed materials in a fresh way, let alone of a sustained statement of a single system, but of a mishmash of this and that that fell together we know not how. All of the documents that together constitute the canon of the Judaism of the dual Torah as defined down to the Bavli exhibit rules of public discourse — rhetoric, logic, topic — though, of course, the rules revealed by one do not conform to those followed by another.

CHAPTER TWO

WAYS NOT TAKEN

Stressing the importance of how authorships compose cogent discourse, that is to say, in literary terms, join two or more sentences in an intelligible way so as to make of them paragraphs, and then link one paragraph to the next to form a chapter I begin with a simple demonstration. It is that different people do say things differently. That is to say, diverse authorships may express the same conclusion or proposition in quite different ways. Not only so, but the differences in media of expression of a proposition derive from differences of modes of thought, so that people may turn out to say the same thing but to have taken quite different intellectual paths in reaching a conclusion in common. Accordingly, as I shall now show, people living in the same time and place and addressing the same problem in the same terms in fact composed their thoughts quite differently from one another. That fact then will point to a single conclusion. The media of discourse, — that is, ways of turning facts into syllogisms and syllogisms into arguments — consequently also, modes of cogent thought and argument, deemed by one party to dictate intelligible exchange leading to the desired conclusion bear no weight in the mind of the other party, which not only states contrary propositions but also frames and says them in an utterly unlike way.

I have at the outset to show that the differences in modes of expression and therefore of thought do matter. One party makes connections between one thing and something else that the other party does not deem to form connected facts at all, with the necessary consequence that one party reaches conclusions that the other party deems utterly beyond the realm of reason. If I can give a solid example of that fact, I can expect the reader to accept as plausible the fundamental premise that the manner of speech conveys one mode of thought and not some other, which requires a different way of bringing thought to cogent composition as well as intelligible expression. Comparing one "paragraph" — that is, sustained proposition, made up of two or more sentences deemed to join together — with another guides us deep beneath the surface of debate, therefore showing us the encounter between the result of discerning one set of connections rather than another. And, it must follow from such a demonstration out of a single important case, people did make choices, quite determinedly thinking about things in one way and not in some other. On the strong foundation of a one powerful instance, I shall lay forth my premise that modes of discourse mediate modes of thought.

For that purpose I turn to the fourth century, a time in which, I have maintained,

Christian theologians and Judaic sages took up shared agenda of issues urgent for both sides. These issues, concerning theological matters, became acute because of a political revolution and therefore bore profound political consequences for each side. Christianity's rise to political power in the Roman empire made urgent a set of questions formerly neglected or treated as merely chronic. One such issue, addressed by Christian and Judaic writers alike, concerned the correct identification of "Israel," with Christians maintaining that they formed the "new Israel," in place of the Jews, and Jews holding that they constituted the one and only "Israel" of all time. I cannot imagine a more critical issue, with more acute and immediate consequences, than the debate on who is Israel, and on whether Jewry remain Israel. How each party framed its proposition, the facts it selected, the connections it made between one fact and some other, the conclusions it drew from the connections — these matters now become entirely concrete.

That is why, in the writings of fourth century authorships, we find the issue framed in the same terms by each side. It therefore becomes possible to compare and contrast the ways in which two distinct groups of writings — representatives, therefore, of textual communities — framed their ideas. When we see that the same issue yielding the same positions (in mirrored images of one another, to be sure) reached expression in paragraphs of utterly different principles of cogency, argument, and intellectual idiom, we grasp the truth of my proposition. It is that a mode of thought represents a choice among alternatives, and the way in which people write a paragraph reveals more than a merely adventitious outcome of decisions on a narrowly aesthetic, for instance, rhetorical, program. Comparing paragraph to paragraph shows us how things connect and hold together — and that portrait portrays not rhetoric alone or mainly. It gives us a visual account of logic. And logic, writ large, is what tells people what relates to what, making connections, forming sense of the nonsense of discrete facts, making meaning out of the diverse messages of the this and the that. Now to the matter at hand.

The determinative fact is that both parties shared the same corpus of facts. That is what permits us to focus upon modes of thought and argument; there was no debate as to basics. Scripture provided the facts common to each party to the argument. The category subject to debate, "Israel," likewise struck both sides as central to the social structure of the world. The legacy of ancient Israel consisted not only of Scriptures but also of a paramount social category, Israel, God's people and first love. And revering the same Scriptures, each group found in "Israel" the metaphor to account for its existence as a distinct social entity. It follows that within the issue Who is Israel? we discern how two competing groups framed theories, each both of itself and also of the other. We therefore confront issues of the identity of a given corporate society as these were spelled out in debates about salvation. The salvific framing of the issue of social definition — who is Israel today (for Judaism)? what sort of social group is the Church (for Christianity)? — served both parties.

The Christian mode of argument finds its representative in Aphrahat, a Christian monk in the western satrapy of the Iranian empire we know as Mesopotamia, ca. 300-350, who wrote, in Syriac, a sustained treatise on the relationship of Christianity and Judaism. His demonstrations, written in 337-344, take up issues facing the Syriac speaking Church in the Iranian Empire, enemy of Christian Rome. The mode of argument as conducted by Aphrahat will strike the Western reader as entirely familiar. He writes in a philosophical way, presenting his proposition on the strength of well-crafted syllogistic argument. We can read him from beginning to end and find in his mode of presentation of his proposition a familiar way of thought and argument, that of the Western philosophical tradition. He presents evidence, tells us the connections between one piece of evidence and the next, draws the conclusions he deems necessary from that evidence, just as would any philosopher. That is why he is so readable. We do not need guideposts to conduct us through his argument; we understand him at first encounter. The proposition emerges with clarity and with power. When we come to the counterargument of Judaic sages, we shall see why these observations matter.

Aphrahat presents his case on the base of historical facts shared in common by both parties to the debate, Judaism and Christianity, that is, facts of Scripture. He rarely cites the New Testament in his demonstrations on Judaism. Moreover, when he cites the Hebrew Scriptures, he ordinarily refrains from fanciful or allegoristic reading of them, but, like the rabbis with whom Jerome dealt, stressed that his interpretation rested solely on the plain and obvious, factual meaning at hand. His arguments thus invoked rational arguments and historical facts: this is what happened, this is what it means. Scriptures therefore present facts, on which all parties concur. Then the argument goes forward on a common ground of shared reason and mutually-agreed-upon facts. Still more important, the program of argument — is Israel, the Jewish people, going to be saved in the future, along with the issue of the standing and status of the Christian people —

likewise follows points important to both parties.

Let us now read some sets of paragraphs of Aphrahat, which he calls, quite correctly, "demonstrations," since these sets of paragraphs come together to demonstrate important propositions, and see how he composes his argument. I outline the work in bold face type, to show the simple structure of argument. I give only Demonstration Sixteen, "On the Peoples which are in the Place of the People."

I. Vocation of the Gentiles
   1. God called the peoples even before calling Israel, Examples and proofs of that proposition drawn from Scripture. [760](320)XVI-1. The peoples which were of all languages were called first, before Israel, to the inheritance of the Most High, as God said to Abraham, "I have made you the father of a multitude of peoples" (Gen. 17:5). Moses proclaimed, saying, "The peoples will call to the mountain, and there will they offer sacrifices of righteousness" (Deut. 33:19). And in the hymn of testimony he said to the people, "I shall provoke you with a people which is no people, and with a foolish nation I shall anger you" (Deut. 32:21). Jacob our father testified concerning the peoples when he blessed Judah, saying to him, "The staff shall not depart from Judah, the lawgiver from between his feet, until there shall come he who possesses dominion, and for him the peoples will hope" (Gen. 49:10).

   Isaiah said, "The mountain of the house of the Lord will be established at the head of the mountains and high above the heights. All the peoples will look to it, [761] and (321) many peoples from a distance will come and say, Come, let us go up to the mountain of the Lord, to the house of the God of Jacob. He will teach us his ways, and we shall walk in his paths. For from Zion law will go forth, and the word of the Lord from Jerusalem. He will judge among peoples and will correct all the distant peoples" (Is. 2:2-4). When he judges and corrects them, then will they accept instruction, be changed, and be humbled from their hardheartedness. "And they shall beat their swords into plough-shares, and their spears into pruning hooks. No longer will a nation take the sword against a nation; no longer will they learn how to make war" (Is. 2:2-4). From of old, those peoples who did not know God would do battle against robbers and against wrong-doers with swords, spears, and lances. When the redeemer, the Messiah, cam, "he broke the bow of war and spoke peace with the peoples" (Zech. 9:10). He had them turn "their swords into plough-shares, and their spears they made into pruning hooks," so that they would eat from the works of their hands, and not from spoil.

   Furthermore, it is written, "I shall turn chosen lips for the peoples, so that they will all of them call upon the name of the Lord" (Zeph. 3-9). From of old the nations did not have chosen lips, nor did they call on the name of the Lord, for with their lips they would praise the idols which they had made with their hands, and on the name of their gods [764] they would call, but not on the name of the Lord. Furthermore, also the prophet Zechariah said, "Many and strong peoples will adhere to the Lord" (Zech. 2:11). Jeremiah the prophet publicly and clearly proclaimed concerning the peoples, when he said, "The peoples will abandon their idols, and they will cry and proclaim, saying, The lying idols, which our fathers left us as an inheritance, are nothing" (Jer. 16:19).

II.   Rejection of Israel
    2.   God not only called the gentiles prior to Israel, God furthermore rejected Israel altogether. Proofs of that fact, deriving from Scripture.
        (322)XVI-2. To his people Jeremiah preached, saying to them, "Stand by the ways and ask the wayfarers, and see which is the good way. Walk in it." But they in their stubbornness answered, saying to him, "We shall not go." Again he said to them, "I established over you watchmen, that you might listen for the sound of the trumpet." But they said to him again, "We shall not hearken." and this openly, publicly did they do in the days of Jeremiah when he preached to them the word of the Lord, and they answered him, saying, "To the word which you have spoken to us in the name of the Lord we shall not hearken. But we shall do our own will and every word which goes out of our mouths, to offer up incense-offerings to other gods" (Jer. 44:16-17). When he saw that they would not listen to him, he turned to the peoples, saying to them, "Hear O peoples, and know, O church which is among them, and hearken, O land, in its fullness" (Jer. 6:18-19). And when he saw that they rashly rose against him and impudently responded to him, then he abandoned them as he had prophesied, saying [765], "I have abandoned my house. I have abandoned my inheritance. I have given the beloved of my soul into the hands of his enemies. And in his place a painted bird has become my inheritance" (Jer. 12:7-9). And this is the church which is of the peoples, which has been gathered together from among all languages.
        XVI-3. So that you will know he has truly abandoned them (323) [listen to this]: Isaiah further said concerning them, "You have abandoned your people, the house of Jacob" (Is. 2:6). He called their name Sodomites and the people of Gomorrah, and in their place he brought in the peoples and he called them 'House of Jacob.' For Isaiah called the peoples by the name of the House of Jacob, saying to them, "O House of Jacob, come and let us go in the light of the Lord" (Is. 2:5-6), for the people of the house of Jacob has been abandoned and they have become "the rulers of

Sodom and people of Gomorrah" (Is. 1:10). "Their father is an Amorite and their mother is a Hittite" (Ez. 16:3, 45); "they have been changed into a strange vine" (Jer. 2:21). "Their grapes are bitter and their clusters are bitter for them" (Deut. 32:32).]They are] rebellious sons (Is. 30:1), and rejected silver (Jer. 6:30). [They are] "the vine of Sodom and the planting of Gomorrah" (Deut. 32:32); "a vineyard which brings forth thorns instead of grapes" (Is. 5:2). [They are] "a vine whose branches the fire has consumed, they are good for nothing, they are not serviceable, and they are not wanted for any use" (Ez. 15:4).

3. God called two, but then rejected one of the two, that is, called the gentiles, then Israel, but rejected Israel. Proofs of that fact.

    Two did he call Jacob, one to go in the light of the Lord, one [768] to be abandoned. In place of Jacob they are called "rulers of Sodom." By the name of Jacob [now] are called the people which is of the peoples. Again the prophet said concerning the peoples that they shall bring offerings in place of the people, for the said, "Great is my name among the peoples, and in every place they are offering pure sacrifices in my name" (Mal. 1:11). Concerning Israel the prophet said, "I am not pleased by your sacrifices" (Jer. 6:20). Again he said (324), "Your sacrifices do not smell good to me" (Jer. 6:20).

    Furthermore Hosea also said concerning Israel, "In lying they seek the Lord" (Hos. 5:7). Isaiah said that his heart is distant from his God, for he said, "This people honors me with its lips, but its heart is distant from me" (Is. 29:13). Hosea said, "Ephraim has encircled me in lying, and the house of Israel and Judah in deceit until the people of God go down" (Hos. 11:12). And which people [of God go down], if not the righteous and faithful people? If then he said concerning Israel, "He has surrounded me with lying and deceit," and concerning Ephraim, "Lo, the sinning kingdom of Ephraim has arisen in Israel," — since the name of Judah is not mentioned in this saying, [then] they respond, Judah is the holy and faithful one that has gone down and [still] adheres to the Lord. But the prophet openly and articulately declared, "Ephraim and Israel have surrounded me with lying, [769] for Jeroboam the son of Nobat has publicly turned them aside after the calf." "And Judah in deceit" (Hosea 11:12) — for in deceit and in concealment they were worshipping idols, as he furthermore showed Ezekiel their uncleanness (Ez. 8:10ff). Concerning them Hosea preached when he called them a licentious and adulterous woman. He said concerning the congregation of Israel, "Remove her licentiousness from her face," and concerning the congregation of the house of Judah he said, "Remove her adultery from between her breasts" (Hos. 2:2). Now, so that you should know that the prophet spoke concerning both of their congregations and called them [both] licentious and adulterous, he said at the end of the verse, "If she does not remove her licentiousness from before her face and her adultery from between her breasts, (325) then I shall throw her out naked, and I shall abandon her as on the day on which she was born, and as on the day on which she went forth from the land of Egypt" (Hos. 2:2, 3, 15). [These are] both their congregations, one of Israel and one of Judah. The one of Israel has played the whore, and the one of Judah has committed adultery. And the people which is of the peoples is the holy and faithful people which has gone down and adhered to the Lord. Now why does he say that it has gone down? Because they have gone down from their pride. Ezekiel moreover called them by the name of Ohola and Oholibah, and both of their congregations he called two shoots of the vine which the fire has eaten (Ez. 23:4). David further proclaimed and said concerning the peoples, "The Lord will count the peoples in a book" (Ps. 87:6), [772] and concerning the children of Israel he prophesied, saying, "They shall be blotted out of your book of the living. With your righteous they will not be inscribed" (Ps. 69:28).

XVI-4. You should know, my beloved, that the children of Israel were written in the book of the Holy One, as Moses said before his God, "Either forgive the sin of this people, or blot me out from the book which you have written." He [God] said, "Him who sins against me shall I blot out of my book" (Ex. 32:31-33). When they sinned, David said concerning them, "They are wiped out of your book of the living. With your righteous will they not be inscribed" (Ps. 69:28). But concerning the peoples he said, "The Lord will number the peoples in the book" (Ps. 87:6). For the peoples were not recorded in the book and in the Scripture.

4.   Summary of the argument: two were called, one first, the other, second, then the second was rejected, leaving the first. The connections between the two facts are now drawn. The reason for that fact is now adduced, hence, first the facts, then the conclusion to which the facts point.

See, my beloved, that the vocation of the peoples was recorded before the vocation of the people. When (326) they sinned in the wilderness, he said to Moses, "Let me blot out this people, and I shall make you into a people which is greater and more worthy than they" (Ex. 32:10). But because the time of the peoples had not come, and another was [to be] their redeemer, Moses was not persuaded that a redeemer and a teacher would come for the people which was of the peoples, which was greater and more worthy than the people of Israel. On this account it is appropriate that we should name the son of God [with] great and abundant praise, as [773] Isaiah said, "This thing is too small, that you should be fore me a servant and restore the scion of Jacob and raise up the staff of Israel. But I have made you a light for the peoples, that you may show my redemption until the ends of the earth" (Is. 49:6). Isaiah further preached concerning the peoples, "Hear me, O peoples, and pay attention to me, O nations, for the law has gone forth from before me, and my justice is the light of the peoples" (Is. 51:4). David said, "Alien children will hear me with their ears," and these alien children, "will be kept back and will be lamed from their ways" (Ps. 18:45, 46), and for the peoples have heard and have been lamed from the ways of the fear of images and of idols.

5. Refutation of the counterargument in behalf of Jewry: God called us alien but will ultimately save us.

XVI-5. If they should say, "Us has he called alien children," they have not been called alien children, but sons and heirs, as Isaiah said, "I have raised up and nurtured children, and they have rebelled against me" (Is. 1:2). The prophet (327) said, "From Egypt I have called him my son" (Hos. 11:1). And the Holy One said to Moses, "Say to Pharaoh, let my son go that he may serve me" (Ex. 4:23). Further he said, "My son, my first born [is] Israel" (Ex. 4:22). But the peoples are those who hearken to God and were lamed and kept back from the ways of their sins. Again Isaiah said, "You will call the peoples who have not known you, and peoples who do not know you will come to you [776] and turn" (Is. 55:5). Again Isaiah said, "Hear, O peoples, the thing which I have done, and know, O distant ones, my power" (Is. 33:13). Concerning the church and the congregation of the peoples, David said, "Remember your church which you acquired from of old" (Ps. 74:2). Again David said, "Praise the Lord all peoples, and praise his name, O nations" (Ps. 117:1). Again he said, "Dominion belongs to the Lord, and he rules over the peoples" (Ps. 22:28). Again the prophet said, "At the end of days I shall pour my spirit over all flesh, and they will prophesy. No longer will a man teach his fellow-citizen nor his brother, and say, 'Know our Lord,' for all will know me from the least of them even to the oldest" (Jer. 31:34).

Concerning the children of Israel he said, "I shall send a famine in the land, not that they shall hunger for bread, nor that they shall thirst for water, but (328) for hearing the word of the Lord. They shall go from the west to the east and from the south to the north to seek the word of the Lord, but they shall not find it, for he has withdrawn it from them" (Amos 8:11, 12). Moses earlier wrote about them, "When in the end of days many evil things will happen to you, you will say, Because the Lord is not in my midst, these evil things have happened to me" (Deut. 31:17). So it was that they said in the days of Ezekiel, "The Lord has abandoned the land, and the Lord no longer sees [777] us" (Ez. 8:12). Isaiah said about them, "Your sins have separated between you and your God, and your iniquities have held back good things from you" (Is. 59:2). Again he said, "You will call in my ears with a loud voice, but I shall not hear you" (Ex.

8:18). Concerning the people which is from the peoples David said, "All you peoples clap hands, and praise God with the sound of praise" (Ps. 47:1). Again he said, "Hear this, all of you peoples, and pay attention, all who dwell on earth" (Ps. 49:1).

III. Israel and the Nations

7.   The proposition of the syllogism: not only were the nations called first, but they were preferred to Israel. The gentiles were justified more than Israel. Proofs of that fact. Accordingly, from the connection between the two facts — gentiles called first, Israel then was called but was rejected — we draw a conclusion, which is that the gentiles' blessing is greater than Israel's.

XVI-6. Even from the old, whoever from among the peoples was pleasing to God was more greatly justified than Israel. Jethro the priest who was of the peoples and his seed were blessed: "Enduring is his dwelling place, and his nest is set on a rock" (Num. 24:21).

And [to] the Gibeonites from among the unclean peoples Joshua gave his right hand, and they entered, took refuge in the inheritance of the Lord, and were hewers of wood and drawers of water for the congregation and the altar of the Lord. When Saul wanted to kill them, (329) the heavens were closed up from [giving] rain until the sons of Saul were slaughtered. Then the Lord turned toward the land and blessed its inheritors.

Rehab, the prostitute who received the spies, and the house of her fathers received an inheritance in Israel.

Obededom of Gath of the Philistines, into whose house the ark of the Lord entered and by whom it was honored more [780] than by all Israel, and his house were blessed by the Lord, Ethai, the Gathite, fed David when he was persecuted, and his name and seed were honored.

Ebedmelech the Ethiopian, the man of faith, raised up Jeremiah from the pit when the children of Israel his people imprisoned him. This is the matter concerning which Moses said concerning them, "The stranger that is among you will be higher, and you will be lower" (Deut. 28:33). They imprisoned and lowered Jeremiah the prophet into the lowest pit, but Ebedmelech the sojourner from Ethiopia raised up Jeremiah from the pit.

Ruth the Moabite, from the people smitten with wrath, came and was assimilated with the people of Israel, and from her seed arose the leader of kings, from whom was born the redeemer of the peoples.

Uriah the Hittite, from an unclean people, was chief among the men of David, Because David killed him with deceit in the war with the children of Ammon, desired his wife, and married her, David received the judgment that the sword would never depart from his house (II Sam. 12:10).

XVI-7. Furthermore Isaiah said concerning our redeemer, "I have set you as a covenant for the people and as a light for the peoples" (Is. 42:6). Now how was this covenant for the people? From the time that the light and the redeemer (330) [781] of the peoples came, from that time Israel was restrained from the worship of idols, and they had a true covenant. Concerning this matter Moses said, "I shall provoke you with a people which is no people, and with a foolish people I shall anger you" (Deut. 32:21). By us they are provoked. On our account they do not worship idols, so that they will not be shamed by us, for we have abandoned idols and call lies the thing which our fathers left us. They are angry, their hearts are broken, for we have entered and have become heirs in their place. For theirs was this covenant which they had, not to worship other gods, but they did not accept it. By means of us he provoked them, and ours was the light and the life, as he preached, saying when he taught, "I am the light of the world" (John 8:12). Again he said, "Believe while the light is with you, before the darkness overtakes you" (John 12:35). And again he said, "Walk in the light, so that you may be called the children of light" (John 12:36). And further he said, "The light gave light in the darkness" (John 1:5). This is the covenant which the people had, and the light which gave light for all the peoples, and lamed and hindered them from crooked ways, as it is written, "In his coming the rough place will be smooth, and the high place (331) will be plain, and the glory of the Lord will be revealed, and all flesh will see the life of God" (Is. 40:4, 5; Luke 3:5,

8. Concluding statement of the proposition:
    XVI-8. This brief memorial I have written to you concerning the [784] peoples, because the Jews take pride and say, "We are the people of God and the children of Abraham." But we shall listen to John [the Baptist] who, when they took pride [saying], 'We are the children of Abraham', then said to them, "You should not boast and say, Abraham is father unto us, for from these very rocks can God raise up children for Abraham" (Matthew 3:9). Our redeemer said to them, "You are the children of Cain, and not the children of Abraham" (John 8:39, 44). The apostle said, "The branches which sinned were broken off. We were grafted on in their place and are partners in the fat of the olive tree. Now let us not take pride and sin so that we too may not be broken off. Lo, we have been grafted onto the olive tree" (Rom. 11:17, 18). This is the apology against the Jews, because they take pride saying, "We are the children of Abraham, and we are the people of God."
    The demonstration of the people and the peoples is completed.

Not only is the argument pellucid. Even the order of the constituents of the case is logical, one leading inexorably to the next and onward to the inescapable conclusion at No. 8. The simple and readily accessible mode of argument at hand — so familiar in the Western philosophical tradition — reveals a recurrent structure of thought: fact 1, fact 2, then: connection between fact 1 and fact 2 yields syllogism A. Not only so, but, as I said, each element of the syllogistic argument is in its logical place, in sequence after the premise or presupposition required, prior to the proposition that depends upon its premise or presupposition.

What is important to us now is to compare the way in which Judaic sages make the counter-case. Their proposition — we shall now see — is implicit, not explicit. While drawn from the facts of the same Scripture that serves Aphrahat so well, the proofs work in a quite different way from those of Aphrahat. Sages' proposition may be simply stated: Israel remains Israel, the Jewish people, after the flesh, because Israel today continues the family begun by Abraham, Isaac, Jacob, Joseph and the other tribal founders, and bears the heritage bequeathed by them. Israel is the family of Abraham, Isaac, and Jacob: Israel after the flesh. That is what "after the flesh" meant. These propositions hit head-on those of Aphrahat (only briefly cited). But they are stated in a remarkably different idiom of speech, therefore also of thought. We find these positions and the arguments in their behalf in — among other documents — Leviticus Rabbah, which reached closure sometime after the end of the fourth century. Parallel to Aphrahat's sustained demonstrations on a given theme, the authorship or framers of Leviticus Rabbah laid forth thematic exercises, each one serving in a cumulative way to make a given point on a single theme. This is not at all the same mode of argument as the one we have just surveyed, even though the proposition implicit here is the same (mutatus mutandis) as that above. We do well therefore to follow sages' ideas in their own chosen medium of expression and mode of argument. For the sake of brevityI give only a few instances. Leviticus Rabbah Parashah Two addresses the theme: Israel is precious. At Lev. R. II:III.2.B, we find an invocation of the genealogical justification for the election of Israel:

"He said to him, 'Ephraim, head of the tribe, head of the session, one who is beautiful and exalted above all of my sons will be called by your name: [Samuel, the son of Elkanah, the son of Jeroham,] the son of Tohu, the son of Zuph, an Ephraimite' [1 Sam. 1:1]; 'Jeroboam son of Nabat, an Ephraimite' [1 Sam. 11:26]. 'And David was an Ephraimite, of Bethlehem in Judah'" (1 Sam. 17:12).

Since Ephraim, that is, Israel, had been exiled, the deeper message cannot escape our attention. Whatever happens, God loves Ephraim. However Israel suffers, God's love endures, and God cares. In context, that message brings powerful reassurance. Facing a Rome gone Christian, sages had to begin with to state the obvious — which no longer seemed self-evident at all. What follows spells out this very point: God is especially concerned with Israel.

Leviticus Rabbah II:IV

1. A. Returning to the matter (GWPH): "Speak to the children of Israel" (Lev. 1:2).

   B. R. Yudan in the name of R. Samuel b. R. Nehemiah: "The matter may be compared to the case of a king who had an undergarment, concerning which he instructed his servant, saying to him, 'Fold it, shake it out, and be careful about it!'

   C. "He said to him, 'My lord, O king, among all the undergarments that you have, [why] do you give me such instructions only about this one?'

   D. "He said to him, 'It is because this is the one that I keep closest to my body.'

   E. "So too did Moses say before the Holy One, blessed be he, Lord of the Universe: 'Among the seventy distinct nations that you have in your world, [why] do you give me instructions only concerning Israel? [For instance,] "Command the children of Israel" [Num. 28:2], "Say to the children of Israel" [Ex. 33:5], "Speak to the children of Israel'" [Lev. 1:2].

   F. **"He said to him, 'The reason is that they stick close to me, in line with the following verse of Scripture: "For as the undergarment cleaves to the loins of a man, so have I caused to cleave unto me the whole house of Israel'"" (Jer. 13:11).**

   G. Said R. Abin, "[The matter may be compared] to a king who had a purple cloak, concerning which he instructed his servant, saying, 'Fold it, shake it out, and be careful about it!'

   H. "He said to him, 'My Lord, O king, among all the purple cloaks that you have, [why] do you give me such instructions only about this one?'

I.   "He said to him, 'That is the one that I wore on my coronation day.'

J.   "So too did Moses say before the Holy One, blessed be he, Lord of the Universe: 'Among the seventy distinct nations that you have in your world, [why] do you give instructions to me only concerning Israel? [For instance,] "Say to the children of Israel," "Command the children of Israel," "Speak to the children of Israel."'

K.   "He said to him, 'They are the ones who at the [Red] Sea declared me to be king, saying, 'The Lord will be king'" (Ex. 15:18).

Nothing is stated explicitly, yet the implicit proposition recurs with enormous effect. There is no explicit argument, followed by evidence that proves the point, confrontation with a contrary argument and its refutation, summary at the end, such as Aphrahat, in the Graeco-Christian philosophical tradition, lays out. We are far indeed from Aphrahat's world of discourse, even while the theme is shared and even the argument at hand is common to both sides. The point of the passage has to do with Israel's particular relationship to God: Israel cleaves to God, declares God to be king, and accepts God's dominion. Further evidence of God's love for Israel derives from the commandments themselves. God watches over every little thing that Jews do, even caring what they eat for breakfast. The familiar stress on the keeping of the laws of the Torah as a mark of hope finds fulfillment here: the laws testify to God's deep concern for Israel. So there is sound reason for high hope, expressed in particular in keeping the laws of the Torah. Aphrahat's mode of argument and manner of making his points now appear quite different, even while the same points occupy the center of attention.

The difference between the discourse begins with the simple fact that Aphrahat makes his proposition explicit, sages here do not. Aphrahat then amasses a range of facts, which rest upon texts, while sages' discourse turns in a quite different direction altogether. It is not discursive but narrative, not generalized and argumentative but allusive and indirect, and that latter trait matches the former. We can open and read Aphrahat, and when we do, we can readily state not only the proposition but also the argument and the connections between one point and the next. To follow and understand Aphrahat, we do not need special knowledge, commentaries or teachers, if we know how philosophical discourse is conducted. In the composition excerpted here, that is not the case. The authorship at hand has collected and arranged completed materials. It has made its point through what it has selected and how it has made the arrangements. Hence, while the proposition is clear, it is merely implicit, and, further, in order to understand the argument, we have first to understand the authorship and its prevailing modes of constructing arguments. The difference between Aphrahat's kind of writing and that of the authorship of Leviticus Rabbah therefore appears to be considerable. The former writes to be read by anyone who can read, the latter writes to be read by those who have been taught to read in a particular way. The former presents a powerful prose-essay, the latter, a rather subtle collage, not an essay at all, but a composite of diverse things (of which I have given only a small part), a kind of poem, if not poetry.

Perhaps we might attempt to outline the stages in the argument of the parashah before us. But if we were to do so, we should find the task considerably more parlous than in the case of Aphrahat. For if (as I maintain) the constituents of the argument are pretty much in the right order and relate to one another as premise, then conclusion, the authorship never makes articulate the propositions that define those stages. When, for example, we come to the statement of how Israel wins and retains God's favor, we see a sequence of implicit themes, in which the argument emerges only if we perceive it. If we read each item on its own, it has its own integrity but plays no part in a larger argument at all. When we see the failure to draw the connections between one thing and the next, we perceive most acutely how different are the connections drawn by Aphrahat, how other the mode of thought behind the manner of expression before us.

Let me impose upon the reader's indulgence by giving yet a second example of the mode of discourse and argument characteristic of Leviticus Rabbah's authorship. The issue at hand concerns Israel's relationship to the nations before God, which is corollary to what has gone before. It is in two parts. First of all, Israel knows how to serve God in the right way. Second, the nations, though they do what Israel does, do things wrong. First, Israel does things right. Why then is Israel beloved? The following answers that question. But it is not presented as part of a systematic argument. It is simply given a position before one passage, after another. If for our part we construct the propositions and lay them out properly, we can grasp the argument.

Leviticus Rabbah V:VIII

1.   A.   R. Simeon b. Yohai taught, "How masterful are the Israelites, for they know how to find favor with their creator."

      E.   Said R. Hunia [in Aramaic:], "There is a tenant farmer who knows how to borrow things, and there is a tenant farmer who does not know how to borrow. The one who knows how to borrow combs his hair, brushes off his clothes, puts on a good face, and then goes over to the overseer of his work to borrow from him. [The overseer] says to him, 'How's the land doing?' He says to him, 'May you have the merit of being fully satisfied with its [wonderful] produce.' 'How are the oxen doing?' He says to him, 'May you have the merit of being fully satisfied with their fat.' 'How are the goats doing?' 'May you have the merit of being fully satisfied with their young.' 'And what would you like?' Then he says, 'Now if you might have an extra ten denars, would you give them to me?' The overseer replies, 'If you want, take twenty.'

      F.   "But the one who does not know how to borrow leaves his hair a mess, his clothes filthy, his face gloomy. He too goes over to the overseer to borrow from him. The overseer says to him, 'How's the land doing?' He replies, 'I hope it will produce at least what [in seed] we put into it.' 'How are the oxen doing?' 'They're scrawny.' 'How are the goats doing?' 'They're scrawny too.' 'And what do you want?' 'Now if you might have an extra ten denars, would you give them to me?' The overseer replies, 'Go, pay me back what you already owe me!'"

Now as to the substance of matters, we find ourselves confronting a powerful statement indeed. If Aphrahat had demanded a direct answer, he could not have received a more explicit one. He claims Israel does nothing right. Sages counter, speaking in their own setting of course, that they do everything right. Sages then turn the tables on the position of Aphrahat — again addressing it head-on. While the nations may do everything Israel does, they do it wrong. And yet if the argument is head on as I claim, the mode of framing it is hardly pertinent in any concrete way. Once again I find indirection, allusiveness, veiled reference, not an explicit confrontation with an opponent and a contrary view.

Let us move a step onward in this comparison of modes of argument and modes of thought. Our contrast has thus far shown us how different were the media of argument of Aphrahat and the authorship of Leviticus Rabbah. But some may fairly claim that I exaggerate the evidentiary power of language. I claimed that how people say things leads us into their modes of thought. Let me now back up that claim. From the surface of argument, we therefore move into the depths of thought. Aphrahat presented propositions and facts to support them, an argumentation of syllogism with which we in the West find ourselves entirely familiar; that is why I could so readily outline the case. Sages not only argued differently; they also read Scripture in a way different from Aphrahat's, and both differences point to a mode of thought of an other-than-philosophical order entirely. Let me show how that thought worked on one important matter, and that suffices to show that the distinctions as to style and form of argument we have now discerned point toward differences in modes of thought as well.

One important problem sages had to work out concerned the place of Rome in the history of Israel. Rome presented a special case, because in its Christian state it was no longer merely gentile, but it also had not become Israel. Sages required a mode of thinking about this tertium quid, and found it in the apocalyptic mode of treating a symbol as representative of a fact, then imputing to the fact traits of the symbol. By treating Rome within the limits of a biblical symbol, e.g., an animal in the vision of Daniel, or in the laws of Moses, sages set forth propositions and laid out proofs for them, not the same mode of discourse or of thought as that of Aphrahat, but highly effective ones nonetheless. For apocalyptic bears a judgment of history, and writing this kind of reflection serves a deep purpose indeed, even within the historical realm. The proposition before us is that Rome looks like, but is not, a valid nation, an Israel, and the framing of that proposition in apocalyptic terms, and the argumentation in behalf of

that proposition, by reference to the traits of the imputed symbolization, bear their own distinctive character — self-evidently different,
medium and mode of thought alike, from those of Aphrahat.

Specifically, the animal that stands for Rome is the pig, and
the point is that the pig looks acceptable, having cloven hoofs, but in-
wardly is unacceptable, since it does not chew the cud. It takes its
place at the end of the sequence of animals, just as Rome (so it is
maintained) takes its place at the end of the sequence of imperial
monarchies, indicating that next comes the rule of Israel. The polemic represented in Leviticus Rabbah by the symbolization of Christian Rome makes the simple point that, first, Christians are no different from, and no better than, pagans; they are essentially the same.
Christians' claim to form part of Israel then requires no serious attention. Since Christians came to Jews with precisely that claim, the
sages' response — they are another Babylonia — bears a powerful
polemic charge. But that is not the whole story, as we see. Second,
just as Israel had survived Babylonia, Media, Greece, so would they
endure to see the end of Rome (whether pagan, whether Christian).
But there is a third point. Rome really does differ from the earlier,
pagan empires, and that polemic shifts the entire discourse, once we
hear its symbolic vocabulary properly. For the new Rome really did
differ from the old. Christianity was not merely part of a succession of
undifferentiated modes of paganism. The symbols assigned to Rome
attributed worse, more dangerous traits than those assigned to the
earlier empires. The pig pretends to be clean, just as the Christians
give the signs of adherence to the God of Abraham, Isaac, and Jacob.
That much the passage concedes. For the pig is not clean, exhibiting
some, but not all, of the required indications, and Rome is not Israel,
even though it shares Israel's Scripture. That position, denying to
Rome, in its Christian form, a place in the family of Israel, forms the
counterpart to the view of Aphrahat that Israel today is no longer Israel — again, a confrontation on issues. I present only the critical
passage of Leviticus Rabbah Parashah Thirteen at which the animals
that are invoked include one that places Rome at the interstices,
partly kosher, partly not, therefore more dangerous than anyone else.

Leviticus Rabbah XIII:V

9. A. Moses foresaw what the evil kingdoms would do [to Israel].

    B. "The camel, rock badger, and hare" (Deut. 14:7). [Compare: "Nevertheless, among those that chew the cud or part the hoof, you shall not eat these: the camel, because it chews the cud but does not part the hoof, is unclean to you. The rock badger, because it chews the cud but does not part the hoof, is unclean to you. And the hare, because it chews the cud but does not part the hoof, is unclean to you, and the pig, because it parts the hoof and is cloven-footed, but does not chew the cud, is unclean to you" (Lev. 11:4-8).]

    C. The camel (GML) refers to Babylonia, [in line with the following verse of Scripture: "O daughter of Babylonia, you who are to be devastated!] Happy will be he who requites (GML) you, with what you have done to us" (Ps. 147:8).

    D. "The rock badger" (Deut. 14:7) — this refers to Media.

    E. Rabbis and R. Judah b. R. Simon.

    F. Rabbis say, "Just as the rock badger exhibits traits of uncleanness and traits of cleanness, so the kingdom of Media produced both a righteous man and a wicked one."

    G. Said R. Judah b. R. Simon, "The last Darius was Esther's son. He was clean on his mother's side and unclean on his father's side."

    H. "The hare" (Deut 14:7) — this refers to Greece. The mother of King Ptolemy was named "Hare" [in Greek: lagos].

    I. "The pig" (Deut. 14:7) — this refers to Edom [Rome].

    J. Moses made mention of the first three in a single verse and the final one in a verse by itself [(Deut. 14:7, 8)]. Why so?

    K. R. Yohanan and R. Simeon b. Laqish.

    L. R. Yohanan said, "It is because [the pig] is equivalent to the other three."

    M. And R. Simeon b. Laqish said, "It is because it outweighs them."

    N. R. Yohanan objected to R. Simeon b. Laqish, "'Prophesy, therefore, son of man, clap your hands [and let the sword come down twice, yea thrice]' (Ez. 21:14)."

    O. And how does R. Simeon b. Laqish interpret the same passage? He notes that [the threefold sword] is doubled (Ez. 21:14).

10. A. [Gen. R. 65:1:] R. Phineas and R. Hilqiah in the name of R. Simon: "Among all the prophets, only two of them revealed [the true evil of Rome], Assaf and Moses.

    B. "Assaf said, 'The pig out of the wood ravages it' (Ps. 80:14).

    C. "Moses said, 'And the pig, [because it parts the hoof and is cloven-footed but does not chew the cud]' (Lev. 11:7).

    D. "Why is [Rome] compared to a pig?

E. "It is to teach you the following: Just as, when a pig crouches and produces its hooves, it is as if to say, 'See how I am clean [since I have a cloven hoof],' so this evil kingdom takes pride, seizes by violence, and steals, and then gives the appearance of establishing a tribunal for justice."

11. A. Another interpretation: "The camel" (Lev. 11:4).

B. This refers to Babylonia.

C. "Because it chews the cud [but does not part the hoof]" (Lev. 11:4).

D. For it brings forth praises [with its throat] of the Holy One, blessed be he. [The Hebrew words for "chew the cud" — bring up cud — are now understood to mean "give praise." GRH is connected with GRWN, throat, hence, "bring forth [sounds of praise through] the throat."

N. "The rock badger" (Lev. 11:5) — this refers to Media.

O. "For it chews the cud" — for it gives praise to the Holy One, blessed be he: "Thus says Cyrus, king of Persia, 'All the kingdoms of the earth has the Lord, the God of the heaven, given me" (Ezra 1:2).

P. "The hare" — this refers to Greece.

Q. "For it chews the cud" — for it gives praise to the Holy One, blessed be he.

S. "The pig" (Lev. 11:7) — this refers to Edom.

T. "For it does not chew the cud" — for it does not give praise to the Holy One, blessed be he.

U. And it is not enough that it does not give praise, but it blasphemes and swears violently, saying, "Whom do I have in heaven, and with you I want nothing on earth" (Ps. 73:25).

In the apocalypticizing of the animals of Lev. 11:4-8/Deut. 14:7, the camel, rock badger, hare, and pig, the pig, standing for Rome, emerges as different from the others and more threatening than the rest. Just as the pig pretends to be a clean beast by showing the cloven hoof, but in fact is an unclean one, so Rome pretends to be just but in fact governs by thuggery. Edom does not pretend to praise God but only blasphemes. It does not exalt the righteous but kills them. These symbols concede nothing to Christian monotheism and veneration of the Torah of Moses (in its written medium). Of greatest importance, while all the other beasts bring further ones in their wake, the pig does not: "It does not bring another kingdom after it." It will restore the crown to the one who will truly deserve it, Israel. This seems to me a stunning way of saying that the now-Christian empire in no way requires differentiation from its pagan predecessors. Nothing has changed, except matters have gotten worse. Beyond Rome, standing in a straight line with the others, lies the true shift in history, the rule of Israel and the cessation of the dominion of the (pagan) nations. These are conclusions that are reached not through a sifting and weighing of evidence, but by an intuitive identification (contributed in fact by Scripture) between a symbol and a thing, the pig and Rome, and the imputation of the traits of the symbol to the thing. No analytical argument can suffice to explain why Rome is comparable to a pig; the sense of the rightness of the analogy takes over. The connection is therefore not discovered, in the way in which philosophy, including science, makes connections through intrinsic traits of evidence. It is, rather, imputed or supplied, in the way in which fixed associations or connections, deriving we know not whence, tell us about connections hardly visible to the naked eye — connections, and therefore also, comparisons. But later on I shall have much more to say about the making of connections and drawing of conclusions through fixed associative logic. The contrast between philosophical and propositional thought, therefore also expression, and fixed associative, non-propositional thought, will become important in due course. We have gone far ahead in our argument.

But we also have come a very long way from our initial problem, which was to show how differences in medium of argumentation derived from differences in mode of thought. I promised to contrast the way in which two authors or authorships composed cogent arguments, that is to say, complete paragraphs, with a proposition, evidence, argumentation, and conclusion. With Aphrahat it was easy to show the construction and composition of a paragraph, an argument and its larger context; indeed, we could see the interplay of two quite distinct demonstrations of his. With sages in Leviticus Rabbah, by contrast, we found ourselves in a very different world. That is a world in which an utterly distinctive medium of expression — of writing a paragraph so that two or more sentences flow together into a cogent statement — conveys also a quite particular mode of thinking, one that derives from not philosophical argument and demonstration but the portrayal of symbols and the imputation to those symbols of traits of character. No one can possibly imagine that Aphrahat set forth propositions, while sages merely created tableaux. Quite to the contrary, time and again we could put — in our own words to be sure — precisely the proposition that sages wished to present. But it is one thing for us to grasp the implicit proposition. It is quite another for us to identify the modes of thought that have generated the medium of discourse and so produced the message in the particular and quite idiomatic manner in which it comes to us. All we have seen thus far is that the logic that joins one sentence or fact to another sentence or fact and so generates a proposition or some other fragment of cogent discourse differs from one writer to another. That tells us that the differences matter. But it does not direct us toward the repertoire of logical modes of making and presenting intelligible statements that characterize the authorships of the Judaism of the dual Torah. To that matter we now turn.

CHAPTER THREE

A PRELIMINARY PROBE:
THE FOUR LOGICS OF SIFRÉ TO DEUTERONOMY

When I place on display, as an example of a mode of thought, thinking through symbols about apocalyptic vision by contrast to thinking in a syllogistic way about a philosophical proposition, I move away from, and not closer to our target for analysis. If I am to make my case, others doing their own analyses must be able to reproduce my results. But one person's syllogism and proposition may well form another's symbolic transaction, reframed into words; and to the contrary symbol in apocalyptic form is surely as propositional as argument in the syllogistic manner. While my simple exercise in the contrast of modes of discourse, argument, and analysis served to make its point, it cannot guide the systematic description of an entire repertoire of logics, that is, the ways of conducting cogent discourse. I have to find a way of defining the making of connections and the drawing of conclusions so accessible that any reader of the documents under study will see them as I do.

That is why I choose to focus upon the simple matter of making connections and reaching conclusions: how people know that the connection between two matters in one case is obvious, in another pure nonsense. When I claim to say how people make connections and draw conclusions, therefore, I seek, for substantiation of that claim, evidence of a concrete and immediately accessible character: the way sentences cohere and make sense, the manner in which paragraphs gain cogency and set forth an intelligible statement. For that purpose, we turn directly to a single text and survey the several answers its authorship gives to a simple question: how do one and one equal two? We want only to define the and and the equal, simple parts of speech, so to speak. Idioms lose currency, styles change, values and even concrete theological propositions shift in the passage of time. What is self-evidently true to one generation is true but merely trivial to another, and urgent issues today retire into a merely chronic state, winning only desultory curiosity for themselves, in hardly half a generation. But the making of connections — that is what endures. For the way in which people add up two and two to make four always requires the appeal to the and, and that is what endures, that and of the two and two equal four, and, too, the equal, which is to say, the conclusion yielded by the and. The logic lasts: the and of making connections, the equal of reaching conclusions. This endures: the certainty that X + Y are connected and generate conclusion Z, but that the symbol # and the number 4 are not connected and therefore, set side by side, produce a mere nonsense-statement. The mind of Judaism flourishes in processes of thought and comes to expression in the premises of self-evidence, more lastingly and more certainly than in the propositions of conviction and confession.

Not only so, but the result of analysis should persist, wherever I turn, and any document should serve as well as any other. Specifically, if I can identify a limited repertoire of what I call logics, through appeal to that repertoire I should be able to account for the cogency of discourse of any document in the received canon. Therefore I should find in any one of them not a promiscuous selection of whatever lay at hand but only a few choice and considered possibilities. Whatever people propose to state should resort to a highly limited range of putting two and two together to equal four. For purposes of setting forth the logics of the Judaism of the dual Torah I have chosen Sifré to Deuteronomy, a rather complex compilation of comments concerning verses of the book of Deuteronomy, because of the range of logics to which the authorship resorts, which are four in all, as I shall explain. Having found these four logics in one document, I maintain that these same four logics persist throughout and account for the character of thought, the mind, of all other writings. The document's authorship presents a felicitous mixture of modes of discourse, in some passages proposing propositions, in others simply making ad hoc and episodic comments on this and that, in still others telling stories, in yet further places undertaking a recurrent demonstration, in one detail after another, of a single unitary thesis. The variety of the document permits us to witness a parade of possibilities of making connections and drawing conclusions, and that is why I have chosen it for our initial experiment.

Sifré to Deuteronomy is of indeterminate origin in time, but certainly coming after the formation of the Mishnah, in ca. A.D. 200, and before the closure of the Talmud of Babylonia or Bavli, in ca. A.D. 600. The authorship cites the Mishnah verbatim and the document is cited in the Bavli. An educated guess would place this compilation in the same general time as that of Sifra and Sifré to Numbers, and a convenience-date of 300-400 is not wholly without justification. But the point, within the unfolding of the canonical writings of the Judaism of the dual Torah, at which this one reached closure has no bearing upon our problem; our concern is with the fixed structures of logic characteristic of its authorship, not with the larger social and political world in which the authorship did its work.

In the document at hand I see four different logics by which two sentences are deemed to cohere and to constitute a statement of consequence and intelligibility. One is familiar to us as philosophical logic, the second is equally familiar as the logic of cogent discourse attained through narrative. These two, self-evidently, are logics of a propositional order. The third logic yielded by the sample-document before us is not propositional, and, as a matter of fact, it also is not ordinarily familiar to us at all. It is a mode of joining two or more statements — sentences — not on the foundation of meaning or sense or proposition but on foundations of a different order altogether. Presenting and explaining this unfamiliar logic of making connections (commonly without drawing conclusions that transcend the things connected) will present the greatest difficulty in exposition, though numerous examples will show beyond doubt that our authorship took for granted the mode of connection we shall define and describe. The fourth, distinct from the prior three, is a mode of establishing connections at the most abstract and profound level of discourse, the level of methodical analysis of many things in a single way, and that forms the single most commonplace building block of thought in our document. It is, as a matter of fact, stunning in its logical power. But, in a limited sense, it also is not propositional, though it yields its encompassing truths of order, proportion, structure, and self-evidence.

Philosophical discourse is built out of propositions and arguments from facts and reason. In the idiom of the canonical writings, we find nothing comparable to Aphrahat's example of conventional philosophical discourse. But as to modes of thought — making connections, drawing conclusions — what we find it no different in its basic logic of cogency. I first give one example of the philosophical mode of stating and proving propositions, that is, repeatedly deriving one thing from many things, then shall offer a more general description of the logic at hand.

Sifré to Deuteronomy CCCXXVI:I

1.   A.   ["For the Lord will vindicate his people and repents himself [JPS: take revenge] for his servants, when he sees that their might is gone, and neither bond nor free is left. He will say, 'Where are their gods, the rock in whom they sought refuge, who ate the fat of their offerings and drank their libation wine? Let them rise up to your help and let them be a shield unto you. See, then, that I, I am he; there is no god beside us. I deal death and give life; I wounded and I will heal, none can deliver from our hand. Lo, I raise my hand to heaven and say, As I live forever, when I whet my flashing blade and my hand lays hold on judgment, vengeance will I wreak on my foes, will I deal to those who reject me, I will make my arrows drunk

with blood, as my sword devours flesh — blood of the slain and the captive, from the long-haired enemy chiefs' O nations, acclaim his people,
for he will avenge the blood of his servants, wreak vengeance on his foes,
and cleanse the land of his people" (Dt. 32:36-43).]

B.   "For the Lord will vindicate his people:"

C.   When the Holy One, blessed be he, judges the nations, it is a joy to him,
as it is said, ""For the Lord will vindicate his people."

D.   But when the Holy One, blessed be he, judges Israel, it is — as it were —
a source of grace to him.

E.   For it is said, "…and repents himself [JPS: take revenge] for his servants.

F.   Now "repents" can only mean "regret, for it is said, "For I regret that I
made them" (Gen. 6:7),

G.   and further, "I regret that I made Saul king" (1 Sam. 15:11).

The contrast between the meanings of words when they apply to
gentiles and to Israel forms the basis for the familiar
proposition before us. We shall now see a systematic
demonstration of the proposition that, when things are at
their worst and the full punishment impends, God relents
and saves Israel.

CCCXXVI:II

1.   A.   "…when he sees that their might is gone, and neither bond nor free is
left:"

B.   When he sees their destruction, on account of the captivity.

C.   For all of them went off.

2.   A.   Another teaching concerning the phrase, "…when he sees:"

B.   When they despaired of redemption.

3.   A.   Another teaching concerning the phrase, "…when he sees [that their
might is gone, and neither bond nor free is left:"

B.   When he sees that the last penny is gone from the purse,

C.   in line with this verse: "And when they have made an end of breaking in
pieces the power of the holy people, all these things shall be finished"
(Dan. 12:7) [Hammer's translation].

4.   A.   Another teaching concerning the phrase, "…when he sees that their
might is gone, and neither bond nor free is left:"

B.   When he sees that among there are no men who seek mercy for them as
Moses had,

C.   in line with this verse: "Therefore he said that he would destroy them, had
not Moses his chosen one stood before him in the breach" (Ps.
106:23)….

6.   A.   Another teaching concerning the phrase, "…when he sees that their might is gone, and neither bond nor free is left:"

     B.   When he sees that among there are no men who seek mercy for them as Aaron had,

     C.   in line with this verse: "And he stood between the dead and the living and the plague was stayed" (Num. 17:13).

7.   A.   Another teaching concerning the phrase, "…when he sees that their might is gone, and neither bond nor free is left:"

     B.   When he sees that there are no men who seek mercy for them as Phineas had,

     C.   in line with this verse: "Then stood up Phineas and wrought judgment and so the plague was stayed" (Ps. 106:30).

7.   A.   Another teaching concerning the phrase, "…when he sees that their might is gone, and neither bond nor free is left:"

     B.   None shut up, none [Hammer:] at large, none helping Israel.

The completion of what God sees is diverse but on the whole coherent. No. 1 introduces the basic theme invited by the base-verse, namely, Israel's disheartening condition. Then the rest of the items point to the unfortunate circumstance of Israel and the absence of effective leadership to change matters. While philosophers in the Graeco-Roman tradition will have made their points concerning other topics entirely, modes of proof will surely have proved congruent to the systematic massing of probative facts, all of them pertinent, all of them appropriate to the argument and the issue.

Now to frame matters in more general terms: In the canonical writings of the Judaism of the dual Torah, represented by Sifré to Deuteronomy, authorships present their propositions in a way that is entirely familiar to us, even though the idiom is particular to the canonical writers and strange to us. Among the four available means of linking sentence to sentence in paragraphs, the first, now amply exemplified, is to establish propositions that rest upon philosophical bases, e.g., through the proposal of a thesis and the composition of a list of facts that prove the thesis. This — to us entirely familiar, Western — mode of scientific expression through the classification of data that, in a simple way, we may call the science of making lists (Listenwissenschaft), as we shall see in the next chapter, is best exemplified by the Mishnah, but it dominates, also, in such profoundly philosophical-syllogistic documents as Leviticus Rabbah as well. Within the idiom of the canonical writings of the dual Torah, those documents bring us closest to the modes of thought with which we are generally familiar. No philosopher in antiquity will have found unintelligible these types of units of thought, even though the source of facts, Scripture, not established social norms or observations of nature, and the mode of appealing to facts, citations of Scripture, rather than allusions to generally prevailing patterns and norms, would have proved alien to such a philosopher. The connection, the process of thought — these seem to me entirely commonplace in the intellectual world at large.

The issue at hand is one of connection, that is, not of fact (such as is conveyed by the statement of the meaning of a verse or a clause of a verse) but of the relationship between one fact and another. That relationship, e.g., connection, is shown in a conclusion, different from the established facts of two or more sentences, that we propose to draw when we set up as a sequence two or more facts and claim out of that sequence to propose a proposition different from, transcending, the facts at hand. We demonstrate propositions in a variety of ways, appealing to both a repertoire of probative facts and also a set of accepted modes of argument. In this way we engage in a kind of discourse that gains its logic from what, in general, we may call philosophy: the rigorous analysis and testing of propositions against the canons of an accepted reason. Philosophy accomplishes the miracle of making the whole more — or less — than the sum of the parts, that is, in the simple language we have used up to now, showing the connections between fact 1 and fact 2, in such wise as to yield proposition A. We begin with the irrefutable fact; our issue is not how facts gain their facticity, rather, how, from givens, people construct propositions or make statements that are deemed sense and not nonsense or gibberish. So the problem is to explain the connections between and among facts, so accounting for the conclusions people draw, on the one side, or the acceptable associations people tolerate, on the other, in the exchange of language and thought.

Another way for conducting philosophical argument — a

way at the foundation of all scientific inquiry — is the demonstration we know, in general, as Listenwissenschaft, that is, a way to classify and so establish a set of probative facts, which compel us to reach a given conclusion. These probative facts may derive from the classification of data, all of which point in one direction and not in another. A catalogue of facts, for example, may be so composed that, through the regularities and indicative traits of the entries, the catalogue yields a proposition. A list of parallel items all together point to a simple conclusion; the conclusion may or may not be given at the end of the catalogue, but the catalogue — by definition — is pointed. All of the catalogued facts are taken to bear self-evident connections to one another, established by those pertinent shared traits implicit in the composition of the list, therefore also bearing meaning and pointing through the weight of evidence to an inescapable conclusion. The discrete facts then join together because of some trait common to them all. This is a mode of classification of facts to lead to an identification of what the facts have in common and — it goes without saying, an explanation of their meaning. These and other modes of philosophical argument are entirely familiar to us all. In calling all of them "philosophical," I mean only to distinguish them from the other three logics we shall presently examine.

We come next to narrative as a mode of making connections and presenting conclusions. In this mode of thought, we link fact to fact and also prove (ordinarily implicit) propositions by appeal to teleology. A proposition (whether or not it is stated explicitly) may be set forth and demonstrated by showing through the telling of a tale (of a variety of kinds, e.g., historical, fictional, parabolic, and the like) that a sequence of events, real or imagined, shows the ineluctable truth of a given proposition. The logic of connection demonstrated through narrative, rather than philosophy, is simply stated. It is connection attained and explained by invoking some mode of narrative in which a sequence of events, first this, then that, is understood to yield a proposition, first this, then that — because of this. That manufactured sequence both states and also establishes a proposition in a way different from the philosophical and argumentative mode of propositional discourse. Whether or not the generalization is stated in so many words rarely matters, because the power of well-crafted narrative is to make unnecessary explicitly drawing of the moral. Narrative sees cogency in the purpose, the necessary order of events understood as causative. That is then a logic or intelligibility of connection that is attained through teleology: the claim of purpose, therefore cause, in the garb of a story of what happened because it had to happen. Narrative conveys a proposition through the setting forth of happenings in a framework of inevitability, in a sequence that makes a point, e.g., establishes not merely the facts of what happens, but the teleology that explains those facts. Then we speak not only of events — our naked facts — but of their relationship. We claim to account for that relationship teleologically, in the purposive sequence and necessary order of happenings. In due course we shall see how various kinds of narratives serve to convey highly intelligible and persuasive propositions. For an example of narrative, I turn to The Fathers According to Rabbi Nathan, rather than to Sifré to Deuteronomy. Its parable is a simple example of how narrative links fact to fact in cogent discourse and further conveys with powerful logic a clear proposition:

I:XIII.

2   A.   R. Simeon b. Yohai says, "I shall draw a parable for you. To what may the first Man be compared? He was like a man who had a wife at home. What did that man do? He went and brought a jug and put in it a certain number of dates and nuts. He caught a scorpion and put it at the mouth of the jug and sealed it tightly. He left it in the corner of his house.

        B.   "He said to her, 'My daughter, whatever I have in the house is entrusted to you, except for this jar, which under no circumstances should you touch.' What did the woman do? When her husband went off to market, she went and opened the jug and put her hand in it, and the scorpion bit her, and she went and fell into bed. When her husband came home from the market, he said to her, 'What's going on?'

        C.   "She said to him, 'I put our hand into the jug, and a scorpion bit us, and now I'm dying.'

        D.   "He said to her, 'Didn't I tell you to begin with, "Whatever I have in the house is entrusted to you, except for this jar, which under no circumstances should you touch."' He got mad at her and divorced her.

E.   "So it was with the first man.

F.   "When the Holy One, blessed be he, said to him, Of all the trees of the garden you certainly may eat, but from the tree of knowledge of good and evil you may not eat, for on the day on which you eat of it, you will surely die (Gen. 2:17),

G.   "on that day he was driven out, thereby illustrating the verse, Man does not lodge overnight in honor (Ps. 49:24)."

Simeon's point is that by giving Man the commandment, God aroused his interest in that tree and led man to do what he did. The explicit proposition is the first point, we sin at our obsession. The implicit proposition is that God bears a measure of guilt for the fall of man.

This brings us to the first of the two unfamiliar modes of establishing connections between sentences. The former of the two — third in my catalogue of logics — is the logic of fixed association. This logic simply does not yield a proposition. That is why the sequence that links in one composition sentence 1, then sentence 2, then sentence 3, though there is no propositional connection between 1 and 2 or 2 and 3, rests upon principles of intelligibility practically unknown to us. Accordingly I have to devote considerable time to spelling out this logic of connection, an exceedingly strange way of defining an and, not only because it is unknown to us, but also because it forms the paramount comprehensive logic in the Judaism that would emerge from the formative age. That is to say, when people wanted to make grand constructions — to accomplish in their context what we know as system-building, whether in philosophy or in science — they resorted to this quite odd logic of cogency between and among sizable propositions.

In a discourse that finds large-scale cogency in fixed association (a term to be defined more amply in a moment), we have a sequence of absolutely unrelated sentences (that is, facts), made up in each instance of a clause of a verse, followed by a phrase of amplification. Nothing links one sentence (completed thought or fact) to the ones fore or aft. Yet the compositors have presented us with sequences of episodic sentences that they represent side by side with sentences that do form large propositional compositions, that is, that are linked one to the next by connections that we can readily discern.

It follows, therefore, that episodic sentences or facts have formed into a composite, even while lacking a shared proposition or making a point all together.

XXV:I

1. A. "What kind of place are we going to? Our kinsmen have taken the heart out of us, saying, ['We saw there a people stronger and taller than we, large cities with walls sky-high, and even Anakites']" (Dt. 1:25-28):

    B. They said to him, "Moses, our lord, had we heard these things from ordinary people, we should have never believed it.

    C   ."But we have heard it from people whose sons are ours and whose daughters our ours."

XXV:II

1. A. "We saw there a people ...taller than we:"

    B. This teaches that they were tall.

2. A. "...and greater...:"

    B. This teaches that they were numerous.

XXV:III

1. A. "...large cities with walls sky-high, and even Anakites:"

    B. Rabban Simeon b. Gamaliel says, "In the present passage, Scriptures speak in exaggerated language: 'Hear O Israel, you are going to pass over the Jordan this day to go in to dispossess nations greater and mightier than yourself, cities great and fortified up to heaven' (Dt. 9:1).

    C. But when God spoke to Abraham, Scripture did not use exaggerated language: 'And we will multiply your seed as the stars of the heaven' (Gen. 26:4), 'And we will make your seed as the dust of the earth' (Gen. 13:16)."

XXV:IV

1. A. "...and even Anakites did we see there:"

    B. This teaches that they saw giants on top of giants, in line with this verse: "Therefore pride is as a chain about their neck" (Ps. 73:6).

XXV:V

1. A. "And we said to you:"

    B. He stressed to them, "It is not on our own authority that we speak to you, but it is on the authority of the Holy One that we speak to you."

XXV:VI

1. A. "Do not be frightened and do not be afraid of them:"

    B. On what account?

    C. "for the Lord your God is the one who goes before you."

    D. He said to them, "The one who did miracles for you in Egypt and all these miracles is going to do miracles for you when you enter the land:

    E. "'According to all that he did for you in Egypt before your eyes' (Dt.

      1:30).

F.   "If you do not believe concerning what is coming, at least believe concerning what has already taken place."

That each unit of thought, signified by a Roman numeral, stands by itself hardly needs proof, since it is a self-evident fact of discourse here. I cannot imagine how, apart from the mere statement of the facts, I can show more vividly that a sequence of utterly unrelated sentences has been laid forth before us. They occur in context of sequences of highly propositional units of thought.

In terms of our language, we have a sequence of sentences that constitute discrete paragraphs, in the midst of sets of sentences that, themselves, compose quite cogent paragraphs of size and substance. These episodic sentences-facts then are deemed to cohere, but in a way different from the manner in which the sentences that make paragraphs (that is to say, facts that form propositions) cohere. The logic of connection of the one is different from the logic of connection of the other.

So much for the example, now to its exposition. We find side by side a sequence of sentences that bear no relationship or connection at all between one another. These discrete sentences have come before us in "commentary-form," for instance:

"Clause 1:" "this means A."

"Clause 2:" "this refers to Q.

Nothing joins A and Q. Indeed, had we used symbols out of different classifications altogether, e.g., A, a letter of an alphabet, and #, which stands for something else than a sound of an alphabet, the picture would have proved still clearer. Nothing joins A to Q or A to # except that clause 2 follows clause 1. The upshot is that no proposition links A to Q or A to # and so far as there is a connection between A and Q or A and # it is not propositional. Then is there a connection at all? I do think the authorship of the document that set forth matters as they did assumes that there is such a connection. For there clearly is — at the very least — an order, that is, "clause 1" is prior to "clause 2," in the text that out of clauses 1 and 2 does form an intelligible statement, that is, two connected, not merely adjacent, sentences.

This third way in which two or more sentences — or whole paragraphs and large-scale units of cogent, propositional thought, for that matter — are deemed, in the canonical literature of Judaism, to constitute a more than random, episodic sequence of unrelated allegations, A, X, Q, C, and so on, on its own, out of context, yields gibberish — no proposition, no sense, no joining between two sentences, no implicit connection accessible without considerable labor of access. But this third way can see cogent discourse even where there is no proposition at all, and even where the relationship between sentence A and sentence X does not derive from the interplay among the propositions at hand. It is hard for us even to imagine non-propositional, yet intelligible discourse, outside the realm of feeling or inchoate attitude, and yet, as we shall see, before us is a principle of intelligible discourse that is entirely routine, clearly assumed to be comprehensible, and utterly accessible.

It follows that the burden of establishing meaning rests not upon what is said but upon some other principle of cogency entirely. A set of associations will join what is otherwise discrete. In propositional discourse, what is said by Rabbi X relates because of the substance of the matter to what is said by Rabbi Y. We have seen, in our catalogue of forms, a propositional form of this kind. Thus the point of intersection of two or more sentences lies not with attributive, Rabbi X says, but with the proposition, what the rabbi maintains. If we for the moment call the attributive clause the protasis and what is attributed the apodosis, then propositional discourse centers upon the apodosis and non-propositional discourse upon the protasis. That is, two or more sentences link to a common point but not to one another, which is another way of calling this mode of discourse non-propositional. The sentences do not form a proposition even though they are deemed cogent with one another. "The dog stands on the corner. Chile bombed Peru." These two facts or sentences in no way connect. And yet, facts of a similarly unrelated character, sentences as wildly incongruous as these, can stand quite comfortably side by side in what is clearly proposed as a cogent unit of thought and intelligible discourse in our document. Our authorship clearly means to appeal to a source of cogency deriving from a principle of connection other than the — to us sole — kind of cogency we can grasp, which is the propositional kind.

The third logic therefore rests upon the premise that an established sequence of words joins whatever is attached to those words into a set of cogent statements, even though it does not form of those statements propositions of any kind, implicit or explicit. The established sequence of words may be made up of names always associated with one another. It may be made up of a received text, with deep meanings of its own, e.g., a verse or a clause of Scripture. It may be made up of the sequence of holy days or synagogue lections, which are assumed to be known by everyone and so to connect on their own. The fixed association of these words, whether names, whether formula such as verses of Scripture, whether lists of facts, serves to link otherwise unrelated statements to one another and to form of them all not a proposition but, nonetheless, an entirely intelligible sequence of connected or related sentences.

Fixed association forms the antonym of free association. There is no case in our document in which the contents of one sentence stimulate a compositor to put down the next sentence only because one thing happens to remind the compositor of something else, that is, without all reference to a principle of association external to both sentences (our "fixed association"), and also without all reference to a shared proposition that connects the two (our "propositional cogency"). Not one case!

To show the full power of the logic of fixed association, quite independent of the fixed associations defined by sequences of verses of Scripture, I turn to Mishnah-tractate Avot, The Fathers, Chapter One. That chapter is made up of three units, first, three names, then five paired names, finally, three more names. That the names are not random but meaningful, that the fixed association of name A with name B, name C with name D, name E with name F, and so on, is deemed cogent — these are the premises of all discourse in Chapter One of The Fathers. The premise rests on the simple fact that these names are announced as sequential, set by set — e.g., the first holds office M, the second, office N — and then in their unfolding, the first group is prior in time to the second, and on down. The order matters and conveys the information, therefore, that the compositor or author wishes to emphasize or rehearse. So when we claim that the logic of fixed association links sentences into meaningful compositions, even though it does not find cogency in the proposition at hand, we believe that claim rests upon the givens of reading the chapter at hand that universally prevail among all interpreters. No one known to me maintains that the fixed associations of the names of The Fathers Chapter One are lacking in consequence. But, standing by themselves, they do lack all propositional character. Let us show that fact. The fact that the logic of fixed association appeals to an available structure to form connections between otherwise unconnected sentences becomes clear only when we see the matter in situ. Let us take up a small passage of The Fathers, so that the point will be entirely clear. We examine The Fathers 1:1-3. I present in italics the apodosis — the propositions, the things that people say, which would correspond to the propositions of a syllogistic, philosophical discourse. In plain type is the attributive, or, in the less precise usage introduced earlier, the protasis.

1:1. Moses received the Torah a Sinai and handed it on to Joshua, Joshua to elders, and elders to prophets. And prophets handed it on to the men of the great assembly. *They said three things: Be prudent in judgment. Raise up many disciples. Make a fence for the Torah.*

1:2. Simeon the Righteous was one of the last survivors of the great assembly. *He would say: On three things does the world stand: On the Torah, and on the Temple service, and on deeds of loving kindness.*

1:3. Antigonus of Sokho received [the Torah] from Simeon the Righteous. *He would say: Do not be like servants who serve the master on condition of receiving a reward, but [be] like servants who serve the master not on condition of receiving a reward. And let the fear of Heaven be upon you.*

Now if we ask ourselves what the italicized words have in common, how they form a cogent discourse, the answer is clear. They have nothing in common (though some may claim they are joined in overall theme), and, standing by themselves, do not establish a proposition in common. As propositions in sequence, they do not form an intelligible discourse. But — and this must stand as a premise of all argument — in the mind of the authorship of The Fathers, which has set matters forth as we see them, those same words serve intelligible discourse. But the principle of cogency, upon which intelligibility rests, does not derive from what is said. A shared topic by itself does not in our view constitute an adequate logic of connection between two otherwise discrete sentences, though, admittedly, a shared topic is better than none at all. But I can offer, in the document at hand, a range of compositions appealing clearly to the connection of fixed association, yet lacking all topics in common, for example, The Fathers Chapter Five, with its sequences of lists of different things that have some trait in common but that in no way point to a shared proposition or prove a syllogism of any kind.

The principle that things are deemed to form a fixed sequence, specifically, the list of named authorities. The premise that because Rabbi X is linked on a common list — a text, a canon of names — with Rabbi Y, and linked in that order, first X, then Y, accounts (for the authorship at hand) for the intelligibility of the writing before us: this is connected to that. That is to say, the logic joining one sentence to another in The Fathers derives from the premise of fixed associations, or, stated in more general terms, an established or classic text. This formulation of fixed associations, this received text — in this case, a list of names — joins together otherwise unrelated statements. What makes two or more sequential sentences of Chapter One or Chapter Five of The Fathers into an intelligible statement overall (or in its principal parts) is not what is said but (in this context) who does the saying. The list of those canonical names, in proper order, imparts cogency to an otherwise unintelligible sequence of statements (any one of which, to be sure, is as intelligible as the statement, "all Greeks are philosophers").

The upshot is that a statement that relies for intelligibility upon the premise of fixed associations, e.g., an established text. The text does not have to be a holy book and it need not even be in writing. It may consist in a list of names, a passage of Scripture, the known sequence of events, as in the Pesher-writings, or even the well-known sequence of events in the life of a holy man. But the and of this connection — hence also mode of drawing conclusions if any — differs in its fundamental logic of cogency from one that relies for intelligibility upon either narrative, on the one side, or philosophical and syllogistic thought, on the other. What holds the whole together is knowledge shared among those to whom this writing is addressed, hence the "fixed" part of "fixed association," as distinct from (mere) free association.

Our fourth logic of intelligible discourse involves sustained and highly cogent discourse in which one analytical method applies to many sentences, with the result that many, discrete and diverse sentences are shown to constitute a single intellectual structure. This logic of joining sentence to sentence into proposition works at two levels, which is why I call it metapropositional. A variety of explanations and amplifications, topically and propositionally unrelated, will be joined in such a way, which is very common in our document, as to make a point beyond themselves and applicable to them all. Here we have a fixed way of connecting diverse things, so showing that many things really conform to a single pattern or structure. It is the promiscuous application to a range of discrete facts of a single mode of thought, that is, a cogent analytical method. Methodologically coherent analysis imposes upon a variety of data a structure that is external to all of the data, yet that imposes connection between and among facts or sentences, a connection consisting in the order and balance and meaning of them all, seen in the aggregate.

One of the most common modes of intelligible discourse in our document is to ask the same question to many things and to produce a single result, wherever that question is asked: methodical analysis of many things showing pattern and therefore order where, on the surface, none exists. Another metapropositional exercise will ask about the limitations and restrictions or broad applicability of a rule, everywhere raising the same question: does the detail of a scriptural case serve to restrict the rule to a case precisely in conformity with the detail, or does the detail of the scriptural case mean to exemplify a classification or type. Another quite different exercise will repeatedly prove a single point out of diverse data, which is that reason unaided by Scripture cannot yield reliable results. Now to make concrete what, lacking an illustration, will prove altogether too abstract, we give an instance of the latter.

Sifré to Deuteronomy CVII:III

1.   A.   "...and spend the money on anything you want [cattle sheep wine or other intoxicant, or anything you may desire. And you shall feast there, in the presence of the Lord your God, and rejoice with your household]" (Dt. 14:22-26):

     B.   R. Judah says, "Might one suppose that if what is purchased for money in the status of tithe should become unclean, it requires redemption [through the exchange with funds, and these latter funds will be used for the purchase of other food]?

     C.   "And it is a matter of logic. If food in the status of second tithe which itself became unclean, lo, that food has to be redeemed, that food purchased with money which becomes unclean should surely have to be redeemed!

     D.   "Scripture states, '...silver.'

     E.   "The sense is, the money first exchanged, not money later on exchanged.

     F.   "I know only that that applies to money in a state of cleanness. How about money in a state of uncleanness?

     G.   "Scripture states, '...silver.'

     H.   "The sense is, the money first exchanged, not money later on exchanged."

In concrete terms,. what we do here is investigate the logical standing of details, asking whether they are meant to be restrictive or augmentative and expansive. Scripture refers to one detail, in its formulation of cases. Does the detail limit the rule to itself? Or does the detail typify, by its traits, the range to which the rule applies. Must we deal with money in the form of silver, or does silver stand for money in general? That is, do we form the rule, out of the case, restrictively or augmentatively and expansively? In answering that question once, we state a mere fact. In repeatedly asking and answering that question, we conduct a methodical analysis. And the upshot of that analysis, throughout, is to turn the details of Scripture's statement of a case into a general rule, applicable beyond the case. Overall, we show that many things form one thing, that is to say, diverse cases conform to a single logic and constitute, all together and in the aggregate, a single highly cogent and coherent statement, even though each of the individual sentences of that statement bears slight relationship to any other of those sentences. What is important then is not the item by itself — the unit of thought seen all alone — but the repeated effect of imposing upon diverse units of thought a single analytical, that is, logical program. Here is the same thing done to something else.

Sifré to Deuteronomy CVII:IV

1. A. "…spend the money on anything you want [cattle sheep wine or other intoxicant, or anything you may desire. And you shall feast there, in the presence of the Lord your God, and rejoice with your household]" (Dt. 14:22-26):
   B. Might one suppose that it is permitted to purchase male slaves, female slaves, or real estate?
   C. Scripture says, "…cattle sheep ."
   D. I know only that one may purchase food. How about drink?
   E. Scripture says, "…wine or other intoxicant."
   F. I know only that one may purchase food or drink. How about things that improve food and drink, such as costus root, amomum, heads of spices, crowfoot root, asafetida, peppers, and saffron lozenges [all:Hammer]?
   G. Scripture says, "…or anything you may desire."
   H. Is it possible that one may purchase also water and salt?
   I. Scripture says, "cattle sheep wine or other intoxicant" —
   J. now what distinguishes these items is that they are produce deriving from produce, growing from the earth, so I know only that things which are produce, deriving from produce, growing from the earth [may be purchased, thus excluding water and salt].

While there is no proposition particular to the case, there most certainly is a recurrent methodical analysis, one that will demonstrate how a great many cases really conform to a single mode of methodical analysis. True, there is no implicit proposition, all the more so an explicit one. Yet the logic does demonstrate a fundamental trait, one that is systemically critical, if, in detail, particular to the case at hand. So that sort of middle level proposition that we see in the forms that demonstrate, through diverse verses or facts, a given point distinguishes the first two logics from this one. Here, as we said above, we find another kind of generalization all together, one that encompasses principles embedded in the foundations of thought, principles of the very structure of reality, — not details of that structure conveyed by propositions that apply to a variety of middle-range cases.

That methodical analysis in fact imposes stunning cogency on otherwise unrelated facts or sentences that themselves have been formed into sizable compositions, showing one thing out of many things. For unity of thought and discourse derives not only from what is said, or even from a set of fixed associations. It may be imposed — as our two cases have shown us — by addressing a set of fixed questions, imposing a sequence of stable procedures, to a vast variety of data. That will yield not a proposition, nor even a sequence of facts formerly unconnected but now connected, but a different mode of cogency, one that derives from showing that many things follow a single rule or may be interpreted in a single way. It is the intelligible proposition that is general and not particular, that imposes upon the whole a sense of understanding and comprehension, even though the parts of the whole do not join together. What happens, in this mode of discourse, is that we turn the particular into the general, the case into a rule, and if we had to point to one purpose of our authorship overall, it is to turn the cases of the book of Deuteronomy into rules that conform, overall, to the way in which the Mishnah presents its rules: logically, topically, a set of philosophically defensible generalizations.

As we review our four logics, we address a concluding question concerning the basic characteristics of the repertoire as a whole. For the case at hand, is the prevailing logic of Sifré to Deuteronomy an exegetical logic? That is to say, do units of discourse that find cogency in fixed association predominate? My answer is negative. I shall now show that the prevailing logic of our authorship is not exegetical but highly propositional. That fact will set the stage for our analysis of the paramount document, the Bavli, which, as we shall see, builds its basic structures on the fixed association provided by the Mishnah or Scripture. I shall show that that document (in the aftermath of the Yerushalmi) went in its own direction, and that taking the path it took made all the difference for Judaism's mind.

But I have gotten far ahead in my story. Let me backtrack and explain what I conceive to be the paramount intellectual structure of this document. The document as a whole is predominantly, though not entirely, propositional. We can in fact "read" large stretches of Sifré to Deuteronomy, as we read Aphrahat, in the sense that we can follow a sequential and cogent argument. On what basis do I make such a claim? It is that most units of cogent discourse in Sifré to Deuteronomy appeal for cogency to propositions, not to fixed associations, such as characterize commentaries and other compilations of exegeses of verses of Scripture. Commentary, strictly speaking, has no need for propositions, though through commentary an authorship may propose to prove propositions. A document formed in order to convey exegesis, attains cogency and imparts connections to two or more sentences, by appeal to fixed associations. It makes no call upon narrative, does not demand recurrent methodical analyses. The text that is subjected to commentary accomplishes the joining of sentence to sentence, and to that cogency, everything else proves secondary. At stake in what follows, therefore, is an assessment of the true character of our document. Is Sifré to Deuteronomy in its logical formations essentially a commentary? Or is it something else? If it is that something else, as we maintain it is, then we fairly claim that the logics of the document define discourse as propositional, not exegetical

Sifré to Deuteronomy takes the overall structure imparted by the book of Deuteronomy and therefore, to the naked eye, looks to us as though it is simply a "commentary" to the book of Deuteronomy. And so it is — structurally. But is that all that we see? I mean to say, does the structure of Sifré to Deuteronomy, arranged, as it is, around verses of that book, dictate the essential character of our document? To expand on that question, I want to know whether the logic of our document derives from the (supposed) purpose of the authorship of forming a commentary. Let me clarify the issue. A commentary's rhetoric, we may posit, takes the form of citation of a verse or a clause of a verse and then amplification of the meaning of that verse or clause, e.g., through a sentence or a phrase. A commentary's logic — what holds things together — along these same lines will rely upon the fixed association defined by the verse at hand to impose order and cogency upon discourse. There will be no place, indeed no need, for discourse to appeal to propositions to hold two or more sentences together, let alone to narrative, to methodical analysis, and to other modes of linking one thought to the next.

For, by definition, a commentary appeals for cogency to the text that the commentators propose to illuminate. True, they may frame their commentary in diverse, appropriate ways. For example, they may comment by translating. They may comment by tacking paragraphs — stories, expositions of ideas, and the like — onto constituent structures of the base-verse. But, overall, the genre, commentary, dictates its own rhetoric, such as we have noticed, and its own logic. The logic of commentary, narrowly viewed, is that of fixed associative compositions. Commentary, strictly speaking, has no need for propositions to attain cogency or impart connections to two or more sentences, makes no call upon narrative, does not demand recurrent methodical analyses. The text that is subjected to commentary accomplishes the joining of sentence to sentence, and to that cogency, everything else proves secondary. At stake in what follows, therefore, is an assessment of the true character of our document. Is Sifré to Deuteronomy in its logical formations essentially a commentary? Or is it something else? The following chart answers the question.

Let us undertake a rough statistical summary of a survey of the logics of the units of completed thought of Sifré to Deuteronomy:

Fixed-associative	159	13.9%
Propositional	690	60.4%
Narrative	61	5.3%
Methodical-Analytical	232	20.3%

More than 85% of all itemized units of discourse find cogency through one or another mode of propositional logic. That figure is confirmed by yet another. Of the propositional units of cogent discourse, 70.1% in fact constitute propositional discourse, 6.2% find cogency in narrative, and 23.6% in the methodical-analytical mode. Since that mode presents not one but two propositions, we find ourselves on firm ground in maintaining that the logic of Sifré to Deuteronomy is a logic not of exegesis but of sustained proposition of one kind of another. Our document's authorship links one sentence to another by appeal to connections of proposition, not mere theme, and only occasionally asks the structure of a verse or sequence of verses to sustain the intelligible joining or two or more sentences into a coherent and meaningful statement.

What holds things together in large-scale, sustained discourse for our authorship does not rely upon the verse at hand to impose order and cogency upon discourse. To the contrary, the authorship of this document ordinarily appeals to propositions to hold two or more sentences together. If, by definition, a commentary appeals for cogency to the text that the commentators propose to illuminate, then ours is a document that is in no essential way a commentary. The logic is not that of a commentary, and (as we saw in the opening discussion of formal traits of this writing) the formal repertoire shows strong preference for other than commentary-form. So far as commentary dictates both its own rhetoric and its own logic, this is no commentary.

Sifré to Deuteronomy is, in fact, a highly argumentative, profoundly well-crafted and cogent set of propositions. We may indeed speak of a message, a topical program, such as, in general, a commentary that in form appeals to a clause of a verse and a phrase of a sentence, and in logic holds things together through fixed associations, is not apt to set forth. A commentary makes statements about meanings of verses, but it does not make a set of cogent statements of its own. We have now shown that in rhetoric and in logic Sifré to Deuteronomy takes shape in such a way as to yield a statement, or a set of cogent statements. Such a document as ours indicates that an authorship has found a need for propositions to attain cogency or impart connections to two or more sentences, calls upon narrative, demands recurrent methodical analyses. That sets the stage for our survey of other documents and their logics. What we shall see, time and again, is that, until we reach the Yerushalmi and then the Bavli, the prevailing logic that sustains the structure of one document after another is propositional, whether the proposition of narrative, philosophy, of methodical analysis. Only with the second and last Talmud do we come to a piece of writing that holds together essentially through fixed association. Now to proceed to substantiate these statements, which address head on, through the evidence of writing, the making of the mind of Judaism.

CHAPTER FOUR

PROPOSITIONAL DISCOURSE

What characterized the making of the mind of Judaism is the movement from fundamentally philosophical and propositional thinking to a quite different mode of thought, which served purposes of discourse — the exchange of thought, the nurture of community of intellect — no less satisfactorily than the propositional kind, whether philosophical or teleological in inner logic and cogency. Here we commence by turning to the first, and the single most philosophical, writing of the Judaism of the dual Torah, and surveying two other modes of propositional discourse, beyond the abstract and utterly philosophical kind, of that initial document. That survey suffices to make self-evident the validity of my claim that the Judaism of the dual Torah commenced in a philosophical, even syllogistic, frame of mind, and that, as already shown, the bulk of the rhetorical and logical alternatives confronting authorships of that Judaism effected propositional discourse.

The principal components of the canon of the dual Torah tend to link paragraphs much as they link sentences. In philosophical rather than literary terms, they in pretty much the same way make connections between facts and also draw large-scale conclusions from those facts. Accordingly, a document that is propositional and essentially philosophical will compose its units of completed thought, such as we should call paragraphs, in the same way that it will join into large scale constructions those same discrete units of thought to one another, with the result, in literary terms, of forming chapters, and, in philosophical ones, of framing a sustained argument on a given problem, for instance, a treatise, a demonstration, a book. That single mode at both intermediate and large-scale cogent discourse is to be demonstrated in the present chapter and the next. When in Chapter Six we see a mixed mode of cogent discourse, we shall recognize its remarkable character, and that recognition will set the stage for the final argument of this book, worked out in Chapter Seven. We begin with documents of a propositional character, some philosophical, others teleological, then proceed to those of a metapropositional and mixed associative logic. First we turn to the most familiar, the philosophical.

When we make points and prove them by appeal to facts and reasoned arguments, we engage in propositional discourse in an essentially philosophical manner. We resort to a shared logic to change someone else's mind about a particular fact or principle. That, of course, hardly exhausts the diverse modes of discourse in which we engage; through other than propositional means we convey feeling, attitude, aspiration, for instance. We communicate through diverse symbols and signals, gestures as much as words, silence as well as speech. But in a religious system in its formative age, which is accessible to us only because it is preserved and transmitted in books, so far as we encounter it, discourse finds realization principally in language, and, in particular, in words arrayed in accord with received rules of sense.

We now realize that, for the document surveyed, most discourse is propositional. But, as I shall presently point out, beyond the formation of the Bavli, the mind of Judaism worked itself out in documents of an essentially non-propositional, rather profoundly fixed-associative logic and exegetical form in character. That definition of the mind of Judaism in its canonical writing dictated important consequences for the kind of thinking that would go forward, and, it goes without saying, also for the concrete propositions that would become possible and even plausible.

The Mishnah, the first document of the Judaism of the dual Torah, ca. A.D. 200, exhibits philosophical traits in both intellectual structure and composition. Some of these traits are of a negative sort. Setting forth a sequence of topics, laid out in accord with the logical sequence in which analysis of those topics would best be carried on, the authorship of the Mishnah produced a document utterly indifferent to circumstance and context, always focused upon prevailing rules and regularities: perfect philosophy, ideal science. Viewed overall, the Mishnah provides information without establishing context. The document moreover does not identify its authors. It permits only slight variations, if any, in its authorities' patterns of language and speech, so there is no place for individual characteristics of expression. It nowhere tells us when it speaks. It does not address a particular place or time and rarely speaks of events in its own day. It never identifies its prospective audience. These mark the quest for regularity and uniformity of philosophers, with their interest not in the case but the rule to which the case conforms. In all of these negative traits, the Mishnah's authorship attained the status of system-builders, constructing a statement of a wholly logical and well-composed character, not merely collecting and arranging the increment of a sedimentary process of tradition.

Let me describe the positive traits of the document, for these too point toward the essentially philosophical cast of mind of its authorship. The Mishnah is a six-part code of descriptive rules formed towards the end of the second century A.D. by a small number of Jewish sages and put forth as the constitution of Judaism under the sponsorship of Judah the Patriarch, the head of the Jewish community of the Land of Israel at the end of that century. The six divisions are: (1) agricultural rules; (2) laws governing appointed seasons, e.g., Sabbaths and festivals; (3) laws on the transfer of women and property along with women from one man (father) to another (husband); (4) the system of civil and criminal law (corresponding to what we today should regard as "the legal system"); (5) laws for the conduct of the cult and the Temple; and (6) laws on the preservation of cultic purity both in the Temple and under certain domestic circumstances, with special reference to the table and bed. The Mishnah is made up of sayings bearing the names of authorities who lived in the later first and second centuries. In the aftermath of the war against Rome in 132-135, the Temple was declared permanently prohibited to Jews, and Jerusalem was closed off to them as well. So there was no cult, no Temple, no holy city, to which, at this time, the description of the Mishnaic laws applied. We observe at the very outset, therefore, that a sizable proportion of the Mishnah deals with matters to which the sages had no material access or practical knowledge at the time of their work. Much of the Mishnah speaks of matters not in being in the time in which the Mishnah was created, because the Mishnah wishes to make its statement on what really matters. The document is orderly, repetitious, careful in both language and message. It is small-minded, picayune, obvious, dull, routine — everything its age was not. In exercising the power of the mind and the heart to find order in chaos and reframe a reliable and predictable mode of being in an age of successive calamities, these sages erected a vast construction of philosophy and theology, law and hermeneutics, all constructed through careful sorting out of detail.

The Mishnah is organized through themes, spelled out along the lines of the logic imbedded in those themes. The six principal divisions, each expounding a single, immense topic, are broken down into tractates, each designated by its subtopic of the division's main topic. The chapters of the tractates then unfold along the lines of the (to the framers) logic of the necessary dissection of the division. While that mode of organization may appear to be natural, logical, or necessary, we should notice that there are three others found within the document, but not utilized extensively or systematically. These therefore represent rejected options. One way is to collect diverse sayings around the name of a given authority. The whole of tractate Eduyyot is organized in that way. A second way is to express a given basic principle through diverse topics, e.g., a fundamental rule cutting across many areas of law, stated in one place through all of the diverse types of law through which the rule or principle may be expressed. A third way is to take a striking language-pattern and collect sayings on diverse topics which conform to the given language-pattern. (There also is the possibility of joining the second and the third ways.) But faced with these possible ways of organizing materials, the framers of the Mishnah chose to adhere to a highly disciplined thematic-logical principle of organization. That is one fundamental trait of the philosophical mind addressing the problem of codifying law, and it characterized, also, Roman practice in legal codification.

A second striking aspect of the document is that the rhetorical traits of this writing match the philosophical ones. Just as orderly as is the thematic-logical arrangement, so well regulated are the rules for stating propositions. A given intermediate division of a principal division, that is, a chapter of a tractate, will be marked by a particular, recurrent, formal pattern in accord with which sentences are constructed, and also by a particular and distinct theme, to which these sentences are addressed. When a new theme commences, a fresh formal pattern will be used. Within the intermediate divisions, we are able to recognize the components, or smallest whole units of thought, because there will be a recurrent pattern of sentence-structure repeated time and again within the unit and a shifting at the commencement of the next theme. Each point at which the recurrent pattern commences marks the beginning of a new cognitive unit. In general, an intermediate division will contain a carefully enumerated sequence of exempla of cognitive units, in the established formal pattern, commonly in groups of three or five or multiples of three or five (pairs for the first division).

The cognitive units resort to a remarkably limited repertoire of formulary patterns. Mishnah manages to say whatever it wants in one of the following ways, all of them ideal for stating propositions, theses, and other philosophical matter:

1. the simple declarative sentence, in which the subject, verb, and predicate are syntactically tightly joined to one

another, e.g., he who does so and so is such and such;

2. the duplicated subject, in which the subject of the sentence is stated twice, e.g., He who does so and so, lo, he is such and such;

3. mild apocopation, in which the subject of the sentence is cut off from the verb, which refers to its own subject, and not the one with which the sentence commences, e.g., He who does so and so..., it [the thing he has done] is such and such;

4. extreme apocopation, in which a series of clauses is presented, none of them tightly joined to what precedes or follows, and all of them cut off from the predicate of the sentence, e.g., He who does so and so..., it [the thing he has done] is such and such..., it is a matter of doubt whether... or whether... lo, it [referring to nothing in the antecedent, apocopated clauses of the subject of the sentence] is so and so...

In addition to these formulary patterns, in which the distinctive formulary traits are effected through variations in the relationship between the subject and the predicate of the sentence, or in which the subject itself is given a distinctive development, there is yet a fifth. In this last one we have a contrastive complex predicate, in which case we may have two sentences, independent of one another, yet clearly formulated so as to stand in acute balance with one another in the predicate, thus, He who does... is unclean, and he who does not... is clean. It naturally will be objected: is it possible that a simple declarative sentence may be asked to serve as a formulary pattern, alongside the rather distinctive and unusual constructions which follow? True, by itself, a tightly constructed sentence consisting of subject, verb, and complement, in which the verb refers to the subject, and the complement to the verb, hardly exhibits traits of particular formal interest. Yet a sequence of such sentences, built along the same gross grammatical lines, may well exhibit a clear-cut and distinctive pattern. When we see that three or five "simple declarative sentences" take up one principle or problem, and then, when the principle or problem shifts, a quite distinctive formal pattern will be utilized, we realize that the "simple declarative sentence" has served the formulator of the unit of thought as aptly as did apocopation, a dispute, or another more obviously distinctive form or formal pattern. The contrastive predicate is one example: the Mishnah contains many more. All of these stylistic traits of the writing underline the philosophical mode of thought operative here.

The creation of pattern through grammatical relationship of syntactical elements tells us that the people who memorized conceptions reduced to these particular forms were capable of extraordinarily abstract cognition and perception. Hearing peculiarities of word-order in diverse cognitive contexts, their ears and minds perceived regularities of grammatical arrangement, repeated functional variations of utilization of diverse words. What they heard were not only abstract relationships but also principles conveyed along with and through these relationships. A recurrent and fundamental proposition therefore was expressed in diverse examples but in recurrent rhetorical-syntactical patterns. Minds and ears perceived what was not said behind what was said and how it was said. They besought that ineffable and metaphysical reality concealed within, but conveyed through, spoken and palpable, material reality. Clearly, the Mishnah is formulated in a disciplined and systematic way, in a way calculated to lay down propositions and lead to conclusions on matters of principle.

Let us now see how the Mishnah's authorships actually speak. In this way we shall see for ourselves the way in which propositions are set forth and demonstrated, in the manner of propositional discourse of a philosophical order. This abstract — which we shall see again later in this book — allows us to identify the and and the equal of Mishnaic discourse, showing us through the making of connections and the drawing of conclusions the propositional and essentially philosophical mind that animates the Mishnah. In the following passage, drawn from Mishnah-tractate Sanhedrin Chapter Two, the authorship wishes to say that Israel has two heads, one of state, the other of cult, the king and the high priest, respectively, and that these two offices are nearly wholly congruent with one another, with a few differences based on the particular traits of each. Broadly speaking, therefore, our exercise is one of setting forth the genus and the species. The genus is head of holy Israel. The species are king and high priest. Here are the traits in common and those not shared, and the exercise is fully exposed for what it is, an inquiry into the rules that govern, the points of regularity and order, in this minor matter, of political structure. My outline, imposed in bold-face type, makes the point important in this setting.

1. The rules of the high priest: subject to the law, marital rites, conduct in bereavement

Mishnah-tractate Sanhedrin

2:1 A. A high priest judges, and [others] judge him;

    B. gives testimony, and [others] give testimony about him;

    C. performs the rite of removing the shoe [Deut. 25:7-9], and [others] perform the rite of removing the shoe with his wife.

    D. [Others] enter levirate marriage with his wife, but he does not enter into levirate marriage,

    E. because he is prohibited to marry a widow.

    F. [If] he suffers a death [in his family], he does not follow the bier.

    G. "But when [the bearers of the bier] are not visible, he is visible; when they are visible, he is not.

    H. "And he goes with them to the city gate," the words of R. Meir.

    I. R. Judah says, "He never leaves the sanctuary,

    J. "since it says, 'Nor shall he go out of the sanctuary' (Lev. 21:12)."

    K. And when he gives comfort to others

    L. the accepted practice is for all the people to pass one after another, and the appointed [prefect of the priests] stands between him and the people.

    M. And when he receives consolation from others,

    N. all the people say to him, "Let us be your atonement."

    O. And he says to them, "May you be blessed by Heaven."

    P. And when they provide him with the funeral meal,

    Q. all the people sit on the ground, while he sits on a stool.

2. The rules of the king: not subject to the law, marital rites, conduct in bereavement

2:2 A. The king does not judge, and [others] do not judge him;

    B. does not give testimony, and [others] do not give testimony about him;

    C. does not perform the rite of removing the shoe, and others do not perform the rite of removing the shoe with his wife;

    D. does not enter into levirate marriage, nor [do his brother] enter levirate marriage with his wife.

E.   R. Judah says, "If he wanted to perform the rite of removing the shoe or to enter into levirate marriage, his memory is a blessing."

F.   They said to him, "They pay no attention to him [if he expressed the wish to do so]."

G.   [Others] do not marry his widow.

H.   R. Judah says, "A king may marry the widow of a king.

I.   "For so we find in the case of David, that he married the widow of Saul,

J.   "For it is said, 'And I gave you your master's house and your master's wives into your embrace' (II Sam. 12:8)."

2:3 A.   [If] [the king] suffers a death in his family, he does not leave the gate of his palace.

B.   R. Judah says, "If he wants to go out after the bier, he goes out,

C.   "for thus we find in the case of David, that he went out after the bier of Abner,

D.   "since it is said, 'And King David followed the bier' (2 Sam. 3:31)."

E.   They said to him, "This action was only to appease the people."

F.   And when they provide him with the funeral meal, all the people sit on the ground, while he sits on a couch.

3.   Special rules pertinent to the king because of his calling

2:4 A.   [The king] calls out [the army to wage] a war fought by choice on the instructions of a court of seventy-one.

B.   He [may exercise the right to] open a road for himself, and [others] may not stop him.

C.   The royal road has no required measure.

D.   All the people plunder and lay before him [what they have grabbed], and he takes the first portion.

E.   "He should not multiply wives to himself" (Deut. 17:17) — only eighteen.

F.   R Judah says, "He may have as many as he wants, so long as they do not entice him [to abandon the Lord (Deut. 7:4)]."

G.   R. Simeon says, "Even if there is only one who entices him [to abandon the Lord] — lo, this one should not marry her."

H.   If so, why is it said, "He should not multiply wives to himself"?

I.   Even though they should be like Abigail [1 Sam. 25:3].

J.   "He should not multiply horses to himself" (Deut. 17:16) — only enough for his chariot.

K.   "Neither shall he greatly multiply to himself silver and gold" (Deut. 17:16) — only enough to pay his army.

L.   "And he writes out a scroll of the Torah for himself" (Deut. 17:17)

M.   When he goes to war, he takes it out with him; when he comes back, he brings it back with him; when he is in session in court, it is with him; when he is reclining, it is before him,

N.   as it is said, "And it shall be with him, and he shall read in it all the days
     of his life" (Deut. 17:19).

2:5 A.   [Others may] not ride on his horse, sit on his throne, handle his scepter.
     B.   And [others may] not watch him while he is getting a haircut, or while he
          is nude, or in the bath-house,
     C.   since it is said, "You shall surely set him as king over you" (Deut. 17:15)
          — that reverence for him will be upon you.

The philosophical cast of mind is amply revealed in this essay, which in concrete terms effects a taxonomy, a study of the genus,
national leader, and its species, king, high priest: how are they alike,
how are they not alike. No natural historian can find the mode of
thought at hand unfamiliar; it forms the foundation of all confrontation with data. For if I had to specify a single mode of thought that established connections between one fact and another, it is in the
search for points in common and therefore also points of contrast.
We seek connection between fact and fact, sentence and sentence in
the subtle and balanced rhetoric of the Mishnah, by comparing and
contrasting two things that are like and not alike. At the logical level,
too, the Mishnah falls into the category of familiar philosophical
thought. Once we seek regularities, we propose rules. What is like
another thing falls under its rule, and what is not like the other falls
under the opposite rule. Accordingly, as to the species of the genus,
so far as they are alike, they share the same rule. So far as they are
not alike, each follows a rule contrary to that governing the other. So
the work of analysis is what produces connection, and therefore the
drawing of conclusions derives from comparison and contrast: the
and, the equal. The proposition then that forms the conclusion concerns the essential likeness of the two offices, except where they are
different, but the subterranean premise is that we can explain both
likeness and difference by appeal to a principle of fundamental order
and unity.

To make these observations concrete, we turn to the case at
hand. The important contrast comes at the outset. The high priest and
king fall into a single genus, but speciation, based on traits particular
to the king, then distinguishes the one from the other. In a treatise on
government, organizing details into unifying rules, the propositions of

the present passage will have been stated differently. But the mode of thought, the manner of reaching conclusions, above all, the point I stressed so heavily in the first three chapters, the mind-set that sees connections in one way, rather than some other, that draws conclusions in this wise, not in that — these will have found an equally familiar place in the mind of both philosophy, of Aristotle's kind in particular, and Judaism, as the Judaism of the dual Torah set forth its foundation-document, the Mishnah.

While the Mishnah's mode of discourse draws us closest to that of philosophy in the Greco-Roman mode, the Mishnah's authorship hardly stands by itself in proposing to make points, propose theses and prove them, set down propositions and make them stick. Quite to the contrary, compositors of other documents, though putting their ideas together in a very different way from the manner of the Mishnah's authorships, conducted an entirely propositional discourse, which, stated in a more familiar idiom, will have found entire comprehension among other philosophers of the age. That is to say, these authorships set forth propositions and proved them. The basic exercise required a clear statement of the proposition, though through ample repetition of cases, the proposition may have been left implicit, and also a systematic demonstration of the truth of the proposition by appeal to a sequence of probative cases. Aphrahat carried on precisely this mode of argumentation, appealing to facts — verses of Scripture — shared between his opposition and himself. The idiom of sages differed, as we shall see in a simple example, but the fundamental mode of argument was uniform.

Let me now give an example of the mode of stating and proving propositions through repeatedly deriving one thing from many things. In the following case, drawn from Sifré to Deuteronomy, sets forth in an implicit way the proposition that Israel is punished, but not wholly rejected, while the nations, when punished, are wholly rejected. The proofs derive from the facts of history, which properly read yield a fixed law of society.

Sifré to Deuteronomy CCCXXVI:I

1.   A.   ["For the Lord will vindicate his people and repents himself [JPS: take re-

venge] for his servants, when he sees that their might is gone, and neither bond nor free is left. He will say, 'Where are their gods, the rock in whom they sought refuge, who ate the fat of their offerings and drank their libation wine? Let them rise up to your help and let them be a shield unto you. See, then, that I, I am he; there is no god beside me. I deal death and give life; I wounded and I will heal, none can deliver from my hand. Lo, I raise my hand to heaven and say, As I live forever, when I whet my flashing blade and my hand lays hold on judgment, vengeance will I wreak on my foes, will I deal to those who reject me, I will make my arrows drunk with blood, as my sword devours flesh — blood of the slain and the captive, from the long-haired enemy chiefs' O nations, acclaim his people, for he will avenge the blood of his servants, wreak vengeance on his foes, and cleanse the land of his people" (Dt. 32:36-43).]

B.   "For the Lord will vindicate his people:"

C.   When the Holy One, blessed be he, judges the nations, it is a joy to him, as it is said, "For the Lord will vindicate his people."

D.   But when the Holy One, blessed be he, judges Israel, it is — as it were — a source of grace to him.

E.   For it is said, "...and repents himself [JPS: take revenge] for his servants.

F.   Now "repents" can only mean "regret, for it is said, "For I great that I made them" (Gen. 6:7),

G.   and further, "I regret that I made Saul king" (1 Sam. 15:11).

The contrast between the meanings of words when they apply to gentiles and to Israel forms the basis for the familiar proposition before us. We shall now see a systematic demonstration of the proposition that, when things are at their worst and the full punishment impends, God relents and saves Israel.

CCCXXVI:II

1.   A.   "...when he sees that their might is gone, and neither bond nor free is left:"

     B.   When he sees their destruction, on account of the captivity.

     C.   For all of them went off.

2.   A.   Another teaching concerning the phrase, "...when he sees:"

     B.   When they despaired of redemption.

3.   A.   Another teaching concerning the phrase, "...when he sees [that their might is gone, and neither bond nor free is left:"

     B.   When he sees that the last penny is gone from the purse,

     C.   in line with this verse: "And when they have made an end of breaking in

pieces the power of the holy people, all these things shall be finished"
(Dan. 12:7) [Hammer's translation].

4. A. Another teaching concerning the phrase, "...when he sees that their might
        is gone, and neither bond nor free is left:"
    B. When he sees that among there are no men who seek mercy for them as
        Moses had,
    C. in line with this verse: "Therefore he said that he would destroy them, had
        not Moses his chosen one stood before him in the breach" (Ps.
        106:23)....

6. A. Another teaching concerning the phrase, "...when he sees that their might
        is gone, and neither bond nor free is left:"
    B. When he sees that among there are no men who seek mercy for them as
        Aaron had,
    C. in line with this verse: "And he stood between the dead and the living and
        the plague was stayed" (Num. 17:13).

7. A. Another teaching concerning the phrase, "...when he sees that their might
        is gone, and neither bond nor free is left:"
    B. When he sees that there are no men who seek mercy for them as Phineas
        had,
    C. in line with this verse: "Then stood up Phineas and wrought judgment and
        so the plague was stayed" (Ps. 106:30).

7. A. Another teaching concerning the phrase, "...when he sees that their might
        is gone, and neither bond nor free is left:"
    B. None shut up, none [Hammer:] at large, none helping Israel.

The completion of what God sees is diverse but on the whole
coherent. No. 1 introduces the basic theme invited by the base-verse,
namely, Israel's disheartening condition. Then the rest of the items
point to the unfortunate circumstance of Israel and the absence of effective leadership to change matters. While philosophers in the
Graeco-Roman tradition will have made their points concerning other
topics entirely, modes of proof will surely have proved congruent to
the systematic massing of probative facts, all of them pertinent, all of
them appropriate to the argument and the issue.

The case, drawn from a familiar compilation, represents a
vast number of instances in which, while arranging their ideas as ad
hoc comments on individual verses, thus as sentences but not paragraphs, facts not formed into nomothetic compositions, authorships
in fact conducted philosophical discourse. That discourse, moreover,

exhibited a highly propositional character, with the voice of the document working through syllogistic argument from fact to proposition. Not only so, but in the writings of the canon of the Judaism in its formative age, entire documents are so cast as to accomplish the goal of large-scale, systematic argument in favor of propositions. They may be compared, therefore, to vast treatises of a philosophical — or a Mishnaic — venue.

One such document is Leviticus Rabbah. Its framers treat topics, not particular verses. They make generalizations which are free-standing. They express cogent propositions through extended compositions, not episodic ideas. In Leviticus Rabbah the authors so collect and arrange their materials that an abstract proposition emerges even though it is not articulated in an explicit way; it is repeated through implicit demonstration so many times that it becomes obvious. In documents of this classification, the ordering of materials is only loosely connected to a base-text and cannot be regarded as fixed-associative even at the global dimension of the writing. Quite to the contrary, the proposition is not expressed only or mainly through episodic restatements, assigned and ordered in accord with a sequence established by a base-text. Rather, orderly discourse in Leviticus Rabbah (also in Pesiqta deRab Kahana and other documents produced still later on) emerges through a logic of its own.

When we listen to the framers of Leviticus Rabbah, we see how statements in the document at hand become intelligible not contingently (in my language: through fixed association), that is, on the strength of an established text, but a priori, that is, on the basis of a deeper logic of meaning and an independent principle of rhetorical intelligibility. The proposition in Leviticus Rabbah forms the centerpiece of speculative argument and it is that proposition that defines the principle of cogency for the composition in which it is presented. Fixed association provides nothing, propositional cogency, everything. Each of the thirty-seven parashiyyot or chapters of Leviticus Rabbah pursues its given topic and develops points relevant to that topic. It is logical, in that (to repeat) discourse appeals to an underlying principle of composition and intelligibility, and that logic inheres in what is said. Cogency is intrinsic and not imputed, as it is in the logic of fixed association. In this sense (and I repeat, I do not mean to speak of necessarily sequential developments), after the Mishnah, Leviticus Rabbah constitutes the next major logical composition of a purely philosophical-propositional character in the Rabbinic canon. Accordingly, with Leviticus Rabbah rabbis take up the problem of saying what they wish to say not in an exegetical, but in a syllogistic and freely discursive logic and rhetoric. The document at hand constitutes not a mere collection of unrelated or random statements, but a set of related and purposeful ones.

Leviticus Rabbah constitutes not a compilation of random sentences but a purposeful and sustained composition, comparable to the Mishnah in its principles of organization and aggregation of materials, that is, in its logical cogency. On what basis do I claim that the document in hand constitutes a single and systematic statement? I shall state matters both negatively and positively. What would constitute adequate proof that we have an anthology or a typical compilation, lacking a logic of either form or topic? What would constitute decisive proof that we have a sustained composition, exhibiting in detail an inner, animating, and encompassing logic? If we cannot falsify, we also cannot validate or proposition. Accordingly, I lay forth what I conceive to be evidence and argumentation to guide us on whether we are right or wrong. The negative: If I wished to demonstrate that a text in the Rabbinic canon comprised nothing more than a compilation of discrete sentences, in no way constituting paragraphs, chapters, propositions and syllogisms, I should begin with these questions:

(1) Can I show that no external, formal pattern governed the formulation of sentences? It would then follow that the sentences were made up with no interest in composing a stylistically balanced and formally cogent paragraph or chapter.

(2) Can I demonstrate that no single issue or problem occupied the mind of the authors of the sentences at hand? It would then follow that the compilation of sentences in no way flowed from a single generative problematic or addressed a cogent problem or proposition. On that basis, I should stand on firm ground in alleging that at

hand was a topical anthology, a compilation of this-and-that, and not a sustained and cogent composition.

True, someone made the compilation as we have it. No one alleges that, crawling across the far reaches of rabbinical tradents, random sentences somehow made their way to a given pericope on their own. Every document reached closure and entered circulation in something very like the condition in which we now have it (making provision for enormous variations in the wording of sentences). But the person who made the compilation followed a simple principle in selecting the aggregation of materials that he gave us: shared topic, common theme. Whether or not through the shared topic he wished to deliver anything more than simply the aggregation of sentences, in no clear logical order and making no obvious single point, we cannot say. Why not? Because the parts do not add up to more than the sum of the whole. The decisive criterion is simple: The order of sentences of such an anthology makes no intelligible difference, because one could have arranged the sentences in any other sequence and gained as little, or as much, meaning from the compilation as a whole.

The positive criteria: Beginning the account of the criteria by which we identify a composition as distinct from a compilation, a purposeful essay in contrast to an anthology on a single topic, we begin with this same point, the order of sentences. In a syllogistic paragraph, the order of sentences matters a great deal. It would not be possible to arrange matters other than in the sequence in which they occur, for each sentence depends upon the other for sense and meaning, one standing fore, the other aft, of the statement at hand. Such an orderly composition in no way serves as a mere anthology of diverse sayings on a single topic. Quite the opposite, the sentences gain their full sense and meaning only in the order dictated by the logic of the syllogism at hand.

Leviticus Rabbah expresses a cogent logic, a logic of form and a logic of substance, a logic of context as well. What has formal cogency to do with logic? The question may be reframed as follows: how shall we recognize — and so demonstrate the presence of — logic? Since logic constitutes what orders and renders intelligible a set of sentences or propositions so laying down the principle of composition for discourse and the rules by which discourse takes place, we look throughout for regularities. Our perception of order emerges from our discovery of repeated choices, first of form, and only second, of proposition. If we can demonstrate a single program of formal choices, we may also try to show that the author or authors of the document — the people who in the end made it what it now is — did some one thing, rather than some other. Then through systematic classification we may describe what they chose to do. That taxonomic description constitutes the statement of the formal logic of the document as a whole. By contrast, if we can discover in a text of the character of this one no repeated patterns in the way people express their ideas — no sustained logic of rhetoric and syntax, for example — we have slight warrant for supposing that in substance or in topical program we deal with a composition, a proportioned statement, a cogent syllogism. We shall have then to concede that what we have in hand is a composite, not a composition.

How the components of the document came into being we do not know. All of them, however, on their own make cogent statements, that is to say, engage in propositional discourse, proving points. The authorship of our document then joined these ready-made materials into a garment of their own design. That is to say, in Leviticus Rabbah we have a composition in which outsiders, not the authorship, provided "completed units of thought" which are whole paragraphs, and which the authorship composed into still larger "completed units of thought." When we speak of these "completed units of thought" and invoke the analogy of the sentence, therefore, in fact we refer not to atomic but to molecular units of thought, that is to say, composites which, all together, make a single point or statement. What then forms the arena for analysis, and where do we claim to locate the boundaries of discourse? The answer is simple. We speak of the parashah — the largest sustained discourse, of which the document as a whole is composed — as the proposition. Then there are thirty-seven of them. Each parashah constitutes not merely an assembly of relevant materials about a topic, but something much more cogent and purposive, that is, a composition that makes a specific polemical point about a topic. The main points of the polemic as a whole furthermore cohere and add up to a single proposition concerning Israel's salvation. So the parts make points and the whole makes a point. And, in the nature of things (since we claim to contribute to the study of the history of the formation of the ideas of Judaism) the point that is made concerns the world to which the framers speak. I therefore claim that the authorship of our document, in its odd and allusive idiom, has composed a philosophical treatise on Israel's salvation.

Aphrahat lists cases that prove how gentiles achieved salvation, e.g., Rahab, Obed-Edom. The authorship of Leviticus Rabbah lists cases that prove how the nations served God's plan, but God always saved Israel in the end. The paramount mode of thought — the taxonomic — requires the making of lists of facts that bear a single indicative trait and so, all together, prove a single proposition, the one that unites them all. One often-repeated list in Leviticus Rabbah catalogues events in Israel's history, meaning, in this context, Israel's history solely in scriptural times, down through the return to Zion. The one-time events of the generation of the flood, Sodom and Gomorrah, the patriarchs and the sojourn in Egypt, the exodus, the revelation of the Torah at Sinai, the golden calf, the Davidic monarchy and the building of the Temple, Sennacherib, Hezekiah, and the destruction of northern Israel, Nebuchadnezzar and the destruction of the Temple in 586, the life of Israel in Babylonian captivity, Daniel and his associates, Mordecai and Haman — these events occur over and over again. They turn out to serve as paradigms of sin and atonement, steadfastness and divine intervention, and equivalent lessons. We find, in fact, a fairly standard repertoire of scriptural heroes or villains, on the one side, and conventional lists of Israel's enemies and their actions and downfall, on the other. The boastful, for instance, include the generation of the flood, Sodom and Gomorrah, Pharaoh, Sisera, Sennacherib, Nebuchadnezzar, the wicked empire (Rome) — contrasted to Israel, "despised and humble in this world." The four kingdoms recur again and again, always ending, of course, with Rome, with the repeated message that after Rome will come Israel. But Israel has to make this happen through its faith and submission to God's will. Lists of enemies ring the changes on Cain, the Sodomites, Pharaoh, Sennacherib, Nebuchadnezzar, Haman. The mode of argument is the same as Aphrahat's, which is to say, a commonplace in Greco-Roman philosophical discourse. From such a mind, natural philosophy, or science, can readily have emerged, given a fresh agendum of issues, those of nature rather than of history, for example.

Accordingly, the mode of thought brought to bear by the authorship of Leviticus Rabbah upon the theme of history remains exactly the same as in the Mishnah: list-making, with data exhibiting similar taxonomic traits drawn together into lists based on common monothetic traits or definitions. These lists then through the power of repetition make a single enormous point or prove a social law of history. The catalogues of exemplary heroes and historical events serve a further purpose. They provide a model of how contemporary events are to be absorbed into the biblical paradigm. Since biblical events exemplify recurrent happenings, sin and redemption, forgiveness and atonement, they lose their one-time character. At the same time and in the same way, current events find a place within the ancient, but eternally present, paradigmatic scheme. So no new historical events, other than exemplary episodes in lives of heroes, demand narration because, through what is said about the past, what was happening in the times of the framers of Leviticus Rabbah would also come under consideration. This mode of dealing with biblical history and contemporary events produces two reciprocal effects. The first is the mythicization of biblical stories, their removal from the framework of ongoing, unique patterns of history and sequences of events and their transformation into accounts of things that happen all the time. The second is that contemporary events too lose all of their specificity and enter the paradigmatic framework of established mythic existence. So (1) the Scripture's myth happens every day, and (2) every day produces re-enactment of the Scripture's myth.

Nearly all of the parashiyyot of Leviticus Rabbah turn out to deal with the national, social condition of Israel, and this in three contexts: (1) Israel's setting in the history of the nations, (2) the character of the inner life of Israel itself, (3) the future history of Israel. So the biblical book that deals with the holy Temple now is shown to address the holy people. Leviticus really discusses not the consecration of the cult but the sanctification of the nation — its conformity to God's will, laid forth in the Torah, and God's rules. When we review the document as a whole and ask what is that something else that the base-text is supposed to address, it turns out that the sanctification of the cult stands for the salvation of the nation. So the nation now is like the cult then, the ordinary Israelite now like the priest then. The holy way of life lived now, through acts to which merit accrues, corresponds to the holy rites then. The process of metamorphosis is full, rich, complete. When everything stands for something else, the something else repeatedly turns out to be the nation. This is what our document spells out in exquisite detail, yet never missing the main point.

Since I claim that the authors do state propositions, I have at the end to make that claim stick by showing how they do so. It is, in a word, through a rich tapestry of unstated propositions that only are illustrated, delineated at the outset, by the statement of some propositions that also are illustrated. It is, in a word, a syllogism by example — that is, by repeated appeal to facts — rather than by argument alone. For in context, an example constitutes a fact. The source of many examples or facts is Scripture, the foundation of all reality. Accordingly, in the context of Israelite life and culture, in which Scripture recorded facts, we have a severely logical, because entirely factual, statement of how rightly organized and classified facts sustain a proposition. In context that proposition is presented as rigorously and critically as the social rules of discourse allowed.

Precisely what sort of syllogism does our document set forth? In my view, it is a perfectly simple one (which biblical historians and prophets used all the time as at Leviticus 26-27): if X, then Y; if not X, then not Y. If Israel carries out its moral obligations, then God will redeem Israel. If Israel does not, then God will punish Israel. This simple statement is given innumerable illustrations, for example, Israel in times past repented, therefore God saved them. Israel in times past sinned, therefore God punished them. Other sorts of statements follow suit. God loves the humble and despises the haughty. Therefore God saves the humble and punishes the haughty. In the same terms, if he is humble, then God will save him, and if one is haughty, then God will punish him. Accordingly, if one condition is met, then another will come about. And the opposite also is the fact. True, the document does not express these syllogisms in the form of arguments at all. Rather they come before us as statements of fact, and the facts upon which numerous statements rest derive from Scripture. So, on the surface, there is not a single statement in the document that a Greco-Roman logician would have understood, since the formal patterns of Greco-Roman logic do not make an appearance. Yet once we translate the statements the authors do make into the language of abstract discourse, we find exact correspondences between the large-scale propositions of the document and the large-scale syllogisms of familiar logic. Along these same lines, we may find numerous individual examples in which, in exquisite detail, the syllogistic mode at hand — if X, then Y; if not X, then not Y — defines the pattern of discourse. We find both brief and simple propositions that make sense of large-scale compositions, e.g., on humility and arrogance, and also an overall scheme of proposition and argument, a micro-, and a macro-syllogistic discourse, with the small and the large corresponding to one another.

What is important is that the logic at hand proves subject to verification on grounds other than those supplied by the proof-texts alone. How so? The appeal is to an autonomous realm, namely, reason confirmed by experience. The repeated claim is not that things are so merely because Scripture says what it says, but that things happened as they happened in accord with laws we may verify or test (as Scripture, among other sources of facts, tells us). The emphasis is on the sequence of events, the interrelationship exhibited by them. How does Scripture in particular participate? It is not in particular at all. Scripture serves as a source of information, much as any history of the world or of a nation would provide sources of information: facts.

Who makes use of these facts? In our own time it is the social scientist, seeking the rules that social entities are supposed to exhibit. In the period at hand it was the rabbinical philosopher, seeking the rules governing Israel's life. So far as people seek rules and regularities, the search is one of logic, of philosophy. It follows that our document rests upon logical argumentation. Its framers, rabbis, served as philosophers in the ancient meaning of the term. And, in consequence, Scripture for its part is transformed into the source of those facts that supply both the problem, chaos, and the solution, order, rule, organized in lists. So Scripture in the hands of the rabbis of our document corresponds to nature in the hands of the great Greek philosophers.

Let me revert to my claim that in generative logic, the Mishnah and Leviticus Rabbah share common traits and form deeply philosophical documents. The Mishnah makes its principal points by collecting three or five examples of a given rule. The basic rule is not stated, but it is exemplified through the several statements of its application. The reader then may infer the generalization from its specific exemplifications. Sometimes, but not often, the generalization will be made explicit. The whole then constitutes an exercise in rhetoric and logic carried out through list-making. And the same is true in Leviticus Rabbah. But it makes lists of different things from those of the Mishnah: events, not everyday situations. The framers of Leviticus Rabbah revert to sequences of events, all of them exhibiting the same definitive traits and the same ultimate results, e.g., arrogance, downfall, not one time but many; humility, salvation, over and over again, and so throughout. Indeed, if we had to select a single paramount trait of argument in Leviticus Rabbah, it would be the theorem stated by the making of a list of similar examples. The search for the rules lies through numerous instances that, all together, yield the besought rule.

In context, therefore, we have in Leviticus Rabbah the counterpart to the list-making that defined the labor of the philosophers of the Mishnah. Through composing lists of items joined by a monothetic definitive trait, the framers produce underlying or overriding rules always applicable. Here too, through lists of facts of history, the foundations of social life rise to the surface. All of this, we see, constitutes a species of a molecular argument, framed in very definite terms, e.g., Nebuchadnezzar, Sennacherib, David, Josiah did so-and-so with such-and-such result. So, as we said, the mode of argument at hand is the assembly of instances of a common law. The argument derives from the proper construction of a statement of that law in something close to a syllogism. The syllogistic statement often, though not invariably, occurs at the outset, all instances of so-and-so produce such-and-such a result, followed by the required catalogue. A final point is in order. The conditional syllogisms of our composition over and over again run through the course of history. The effort is to demonstrate that the rule at hand applies at all times, under all circumstances. Why so? It is because the conditional syllogism must serve under all temporal circumstances. The recurrent listing of events subject to a single rule runs as often as possible through the course of all of human history, from creation to the fourth monarchy (Rome), which, everyone knows, is the end of time prior to the age that is coming. Accordingly, the veracity of Rabbinic conditional arguments depends over and over again on showing that the condition holds at all times.

To summarize: the proposition of the syllogistic argument at hand derives from clear statements of Scripture, the conditional part: if X, then Y; if not X, then not Y. Leviticus 26 (which occupies strikingly slight attention in our composition) states explicitly that if the Israelites keep God's rules, they will prosper, and if not, they will suffer. The viewpoint is commonplace, but its appearance at Leviticus in particular validates the claim that it is topically available to our authors. The two further stages in the encompassing logic of the document do represent a step beyond the simple and commonplace theorem. The first is the construction of the molecular argument, encompassing a broad range of subjects. The second, and the more important of the two, is the insistence of the temporal character of the list. That is why the recurrent reference to sequences of figures, events, or actions, all listed in accord with a monothetic definitive trait, forms so central a component in the argument of the document as a whole.

The Mishnah too composes its arguments through the laying down of basic principles — syllogisms — sustained by lists of specific instances in the validation and clarification of those principles. So too the authors of Leviticus Rabbah collect and arrange, since they do not propose to invent facts, but to interpret them by discovering the rules the facts obey. The facts with which they work are indifferently Scriptural or contemporary (though mostly the former). The propositions they propose to demonstrate through these facts, however, are eternal. So, in a word, Leviticus Rabbah takes up the modes of thought and argumentation characteristic of the Mishnah (and, in one measure or other, of the larger Greco-Roman philosophical setting) and accomplishes the logically necessary task of applying them to society. Speaking of society, the authors turn to, among other records, the history-book, Scripture, which provides examples of the special laws governing Israel, the physics of Israel's fate. In Scripture, but not only there, the authors find rules and apply them to their own day. Greek science focused upon physics.

Then the laws of Israel's salvation serve as the physics of the sages. But Greek science derived facts and built theorems on the basis of other sources besides physics; the philosophers also, after all, studied ethnography, ethics, politics, and history. For the sages at hand, along these same lines, parables, exemplary tales, and completed paragraphs of thought deriving from other sources (not to exclude the Mishnah, Tosefta, Sifra, Genesis Rabbah and such literary compositions that had been made ready for the Talmud of the Land of Israel) — these too make their contribution of data subject to analysis. All of these sources of truth, all together, were directed toward the discovery of philosophical laws for the understanding of Israel's life, now and in the age to come.

What we have in Leviticus Rabbah, therefore, is the result of the mode of thought not of prophets or historians, but of philosophers and scientists. The framers propose not to lay down, but to discover, rules governing Israel's life. As we find the rules of nature by identifying and classifying facts of natural life, so we find rules of society by identifying and classifying the facts of Israel's social life. In both modes of inquiry we make sense of things by bringing together like specimens and finding out whether they form a species, then bringing together like species and finding out whether they form a genus — in all, classifying data and identifying the rules that make possible the classification. That sort of thinking lies at the deepest level of list-making, which is work of offering a proposition and facts (for social rules) as much as a genus and its species (for rules of nature). Once discovered, the social rules of Israel's national life of course yield explicit statements, such as that God hates the arrogant and loves the humble. As we have seen, the readily-assembled syllogism follows: if one is arrogant, God will hate him, and if he is humble, God will love him. The logical status of these statements, in context, is as secure and unassailable as the logical status of statements about physics, ethics, or politics, as these emerge in philosophical thought. What differentiates the statements is not their logical status — as sound, scientific philosophy — but only their subject matter, on the one side, and distinctive rhetoric, on the other.

While the authorships of the Mishnah and Leviticus Rabbah present propositions by establishing connections syllogistically and drawing conclusions philosophically, the canon of the Judaism of the dual Torah contained systematic efforts at stating propositions (whether explicitly, whether implicitly) in yet another, entirely familiar manner. It was through narrative. Narrative joins one fact to the next to form a cogent whole and set forth a proposition, but it does so in a logic different from the philosophical. In general, a narrative will see a connection between fact A and fact B because of what happens then, which is fact C. Fact A comes first, then fact, B, and because of that order, e.g., on account of the tension created between fact A and fact B, fact C comes about. The appeal to causation, e.g., to the resolution of tension, marks the logic of connection as not propositional, demonstrated syllogistically, but rather, teleological, demonstrated purposively. But the highly propositional consequence of narrative cannot escape our notice, and, when we examine a variety of stories in the canon of the dual Torah, we find that the teleological logic of connection functions as efficiently as the philosophical-syllogistic in setting forth lucidly presented and persuasively proved propositions.

Philosophical logic is not the only kind that produces propositional discourse. Narrative logic, which we considered above, serves to establish propositions. For the purpose of a brief demonstration of the working of the mind of Judaism through narrative presentation of proposition, I turn to The Fathers According to Rabbi Nathan, a document of indeterminate authorship and origin, finding its place well within the orbit of the Talmud of Babylonia and therefore to be situated, as a rough guess, in the fifth or sixth centuries. The authorship of that document received The Fathers, a collection of aphorisms, and added to it a layer of stories about the sages to whom the aphorisms were assigned. In that layer of stories, the later authorship registered points and established propositions that transformed the message, delivered all together and in the aggregate, of the earlier document. That fact makes The Fathers According to Rabbi Nathan a particularly valuable source of examples of the use of stories to set forth and demonstrate propositions.

The authorship of The Fathers had presented the message of sages solely in aphoristic form. Apophthegms bore the entire weight of that authorship's propositions, and — quite consistently — what made one saying cogent with others fore and aft was, as we saw in Chapter Three, solely the position of the authority behind that saying: here, not there was defined by this authority, not that authority. By contrast, we find no fewer than four types of narrative in The Fathers According to Rabbi Nathan, precedent, precipitant, parable, and story (classified by topic, scriptural or sagacious, with each classification exhibiting its distinctive narrative conventions). The authorship of The Fathers had of course fully acknowledged the importance of the past. But they did not retell and include in their composition the scriptural stories of what had happened long ago. They understood that their predecessors lived exemplary lives. But they did not narrate stories about sages. The authorship of The Fathers According to Rabbi Nathan clearly found inadequate the mode of intelligible discourse and the medium of expression selected by the framers of the document they chose to extend.

The later writers possessed a message they deemed integral to that unfolding Torah of Moses at Sinai. They resorted to a mode of intelligible discourse, narrative, that conveyed propositions with great clarity, deeming the medium — again, narrative — a vehicle for conveying propositions from heart to heart. Not only so, but among the narratives utilized in their composition, they selected one for closest attention and narrative development. The sage-story took pride of place in its paramount position in The Fathers According to Rabbi Nathan, and that same sub-classification of narrative bore messages conveyed, in the document before us, in no other medium. The framers of the Fathers According to Rabbi Nathan made ample use of formerly neglected matters of intellect, aesthetics, and theology, specifically, to compose their ideas through a mode of thought and cogent thought, so as to construct intelligible discourse through a medium, meant to speak with immediacy and power to convey a message of critical urgency. The sage-story — that is, a story in which a sage of the Mishnah is the hero and actor — exhibits these traits:

[1] the story about a sage has a beginning, middle, and end, and the story about a sage also rests not only on verbal exchanges ("he said to him..., he said to him..."), but on (described) action.

[2] the story about a sage unfolds from a point of tension and conflict to a clear resolution and remission of the conflict.

[3] the story about a sage rarely invokes a verse of Scripture and never serves to prove a proposition concerning the meaning of a verse of Scripture.

The traits of stories about scriptural figures and themes prove opposite:

[1] in the story about a scriptural hero there is no beginning, middle, and end, and little action. The burden of the narrative is carried by "he said to him..., he said to him...." Described action is rare and plays slight role in the unfolding of the narrative. Often the narrative con-

sists of little more than a setting for a saying, and the point of the narrative is conveyed not through what is told but through the cited saying.

[2] the story about a scriptural hero is worked out as a tableau, with description of the components of the stationary tableau placed at the center. There is little movement, no point of tension that is resolved.

[3] the story about a scriptural hero always invokes verses from Scripture and makes the imputation of meaning to those verses the center of interest.

Sage-stories attend to only four topics: the sage's beginning in Torah-study, his character and his deeds in relationship to the Torah, the role of the sage in important historical events, and at the end, the death of sages. A list of the topics that are neglected, for example, the sage's childhood and wonderful precociousness in Torah-study, the sage's supernatural deeds, the sage's everyday administration of the community's affairs, the sage's life with other sages and with disciples — such a list could be extended over many pages. But it suffices to notice that our document has chosen a highly restricted list of topics, but then differentiated, within these topics, by telling quite diverse stories about different sages as to their origins, deaths, and the like. The upshot is that when the authorship of The Fathers According to Rabbi Nathan resorted to narrative in general and story-telling in particular, with special attention to sage-stories, those compositors had in mind a very particular purpose and message indeed. There was nothing random or episodic in their choices of topics, and the medium of story-telling served the message conveyed by the story set forth in our composition. Not only so, but the logic that joined fact to fact to make a cogent set of sentences, and that generated a given set of conclusions, proved particular, in this document, to sage-stories.

Let me establish this claim by attending to a single important story and showing that it presents a proposition, and does so with great cogency and power. It concerns a principal historical event and conveys what sages in our document wish to state as their position on that event: a proposition concerning the destruction of the second

Temple of Jerusalem in A.D. 70. All sage-stories in the Fathers According to Rabbi Nathan that deal not with the lives and deeds of sages concern the one large historical question facing Israel: its history in this world and destiny in the world to come. History finds its definition in a single event: the encounter with Rome, involving two aspects, first, the destruction of the Temple and the sages' role in dealing with that matter; second, the (associated, consequent) repression of Torah-sages and their study. Israel's history in this world works itself out in the encounter with Rome, Israel's counterpart and opposite, and that history in the world coming soon will see a reversal of roles. The centrality of study of the Torah in securing Israel's future forms the leitmotif of the stories at hand. The authorship of The Fathers According to Rabbi Nathan presents a story about the centrality of the sage and Torah-study in the history of Israel by setting Yohanan ben Zakkai into the center of the tale of the Roman conquest of Jerusalem:

IV:VI.

1   A.   Now when Vespasian came to destroy Jerusalem, he said to [the inhabitants of the city,] "Idiots! why do you want to destroy this city and burn the house of the sanctuary? For what do I want of you, except that you send me a bow or an arrow [as marks of submission to my rule], and I shall go on my way."

     B.   They said to him, "Just as we sallied out against the first two who came before you and killed them, so shall we sally out and kill you."

     C.   When Rabban Yohanan ben Zakkai heard, he proclaimed to the men of Jerusalem, saying to them, "My sons, why do you want to destroy this city and burn the house of the sanctuary? For what does he want of you, except that you send him a bow or an arrow, and he will go on his way."

     D.   They said to him, "Just as we sallied out against the first two who came before him and killed them, so shall we sally out and kill him."

     E.   Vespasian had stationed men near the walls of the city, and whatever they heard, they would write on an arrow and shoot out over the wall. [They reported] that Rabban Yohanan ben Zakkai was a loyalist of Caesar's.

     F.   After Rabban Yohanan ben Zakkai had spoken to them one day, a second, and a third, and the people did not accept his counsel, he sent and called his disciples, R. Eliezer and R. Joshua, saying to them, "My sons, go and get me out of here. Make me an ark and I shall go to sleep in it."

     G.   R. Eliezer took the head and R. Joshua the feet, and toward sunset they carried him until they came to the gates of Jerusalem.

H.   The gate keepers said to them, "Who is this?"

I.   They said to him, "It is a corpse. Do you not know that a corpse is not kept overnight in Jerusalem."

J.   They said to them, "If it is a corpse, take him out," so they took him out and brought him out at sunset, until they came to Vespasian.

K.   They opened the ark and he stood before him.

L.   He said to him, "Are you Rabban Yohanan ben Zakkai? Indicate what I should give you."

M.   He said to him, "I ask from you only Yavneh, to which I shall go, and where I shall teach my disciples, establish prayer [Goldin: a prayer house], and carry out all of the religious duties."

N.   He said to him, "Go and do whatever you want."

O.   He said to him, "Would you mind if I said something to you."

P.   He said to him, "Go ahead."]

Q.   He said to him, "Lo, you are going to be made sovereign."

R.   He said to him, "How do you know?

S.   He said to him, "It is a tradition of ours that the house of the sanctuary will be given over not into the power of a commoner but of a king, for it is said, And he shall cut down the thickets of the forest with iron, and Lebanon [which refers to the Temple] shall fall by a mighty one (Is. 10:34)."

T.   People say that not a day, two or three passed before a delegation came to him from his city indicating that the [former] Caesar had died and they had voted for him to ascend the throne.

U.   They brought him a [Goldin:] catapult and drew it up against the wall of Jerusalem.

V.   They brought him cedar beams and put them into the catapult, and he struck them against the wall until a breach had been made in it. They brought the head of a pig and put it into the catapult and tossed it toward the limbs that were on the Temple altar.

W.   At that moment Jerusalem was captured.

X.   Rabban Yohanan ben Zakkai was in session and with trembling was looking outward, in the way that Eli had sat and waited: Lo, Eli sat upon his seat by the wayside watching, for his heart trembled for the ark of God (1 Sam. 4:13).

Y.   When Rabban Yohanan ben Zakkai heard that Jerusalem had been destroyed and the house of the sanctuary burned in flames, he tore his garments, and his disciples tore their garments, and they wept and cried and mourned.

The story unfolds in a smooth way from beginning to end. The proposition of the story is that the sage and the emperor are in the balance, the might of the Torah as against the might of Rome, and the sage in the end will triumph through the Torah. The story therefore serves, overall, as an account of the power of the Torah to lead Israel through historical crises. Specifically, the story-teller at three points — [1] the comparison of Vespasian and the Jewish troops and Yohanan and the Jewish troops, [2] Vespasian and Yohanan in their director encounter, then at the end, [3] with the destruction itself — places the sage into the scale against the emperor, Israel against Rome. Then the Torah makes the difference, for, in the end, Israel will outweigh Rome. The story's themes all form part of the larger theme of Torah-learning. The centerpiece is Yohanan's knowledge that the Temple is going to be destroyed. This he acquired in two ways. First of all, his observation of the conduct of the Israelite army led him to that conclusion. But, second and more important, his knowledge of the Torah told him the deeper meaning of the event, which was in two parts. The one side had Rome get a new emperor. The other, and counterpart, side had Israel get its program for the period beyond the destruction.

The opening unit of the story, A-T, seems to me seamless. I can point to no element that can have been omitted without seriously damaging the integrity of the story. I see no intrusions of any kind. If that is a correct judgment, then the climax must come only at S, confirmed by T and what follows. That is to say, it is the power of the sage to know the future because of his knowledge of the Torah. Establishing a place for the teaching of disciples and the performance of other holy duties forms a substrate of the same central theme. And yet, deeper still, lies the theme of the counterpart and opposite: Israel and Rome, sage and emperor. That motif occurs, to begin with at A, C, which have Vespasian and Yohanan say precisely the same thing, with one difference. Vespasian calls the Jewish army "idiots," and Yohanan calls the troops, "my sons." Otherwise the statements are the same. And the replies, B, D, are also the same. So the first episode sets the emperor and the sage up as opposites and counterparts.

The second episode has the people unwilling to listen to the sage — the emperor has no role here — leading the sage to conclude that it is time to "make an ark and go to sleep in it." If I had to choose a point of reference, it would be not the sleep of death — then Yohanan would have wanted a bier — but the ark of Noah. Yohanan then forms the counterpart, in the story-teller's choice of the word at hand, to Noah, who will save the world beyond the coming deluge. I would then see F-G as a chapter in a complete story. E, on the one side, and H-J, on the other, link that cogent chapter to the larger context. E prepares us to understand why Vespasian recognizes Yohanan, an important detail, added precisely where it had to come, and H-J form the necessary bridge to what is coming.

The third component of the unitary story again places Vespasian in the balance against Yohanan. Now Yohanan tells Vespasian what is going to happen. Each party rises to power as a direct outcome of the destruction of the Temple: sage vs. emperor, one in the scale against the other. The colloquy with Vespasian, L-S, form the only part of the story to rely upon a narrative consisting of "he said to him...he said to him...." The point, of course, is clear as already stated. Then comes the necessary denouement, in two parts. First, the Temple actually was destroyed; we are told how, T-W, second, Yohanan responded in mourning, X-Y. Here too we have that same counterpart and opposite: Rome, then Israel, with Israel represented by the sage, Rome by the emperor.

That the story before us is so told as to convey a very particular proposition becomes still clearer when we compare it to the way in which a different story-teller treated the same topic (in inappropriate, historical language: the same event), namely, the sage and the destruction of the Temple. The story occurs at Babylonian Talmud tractate Gittin 56a-b, and I provide a paraphrase, which suffices. Where the language of the text is cited, it is in the translation of M. Simon, *The Babylonian Talmud. Gittin*, (London, 1948: Soncino Press) pp. 254-260. Where called for, I insert the pertinent parallels of the story as it occurs in The Fathers According to Rabbi Nathan to underline the contrast.

1. Superscription: R. Yohanan said, "What is illustrative of the verse, Happy is the man who fears always, but he who hardens his heart shall fall into mischief (Prov, 28:14)? The destruction of Jerusalem came through Qamsa and Bar Qamsa; the destruction of Tur Malka through a cock and a hen; the destruction of Betar through the shaft of a leather."

2. Because of the contention between Qamsa and Bar Qamsa: the one gave a party and did not invite the other, who came anyhow and got thrown out. The sages present did not object. The injured party informed against them, saying, the Jews are rebelling against you. This led to the destruction of the Temple.

3. The emperor sent Nero, who produced an omen to indicate the city will fall. He had a boy repeat the verse of Scripture he had just learned, which was Ez. 25:14, predicting that Edom-Rome would destroy the Temple. He became a proselyte, from whom Meir was descended.

4. He sent against them Vespasian. Three wealthy men in the city, Naqdimon, Ben Kalba Shabua, and Ben Sisis Hakkesset were there. Each had enough to keep the city in food, drink, and fuel. The sages in the city wanted to make peace with the Romans. The zealots would not agree, but burned the stories of wheat and barley, so producing a famine.

5. Martha daughter of Boethius, rich woman, could not get food. She ultimate went without her shoes to find food, some dung stuck to her foot, and Yohanan b. Zakkai invoked the verse, The tender and delicate woman which would not adventure to set the sole of her foot upon the ground (Deut. 28:5).

6. Sadoq fasted for forty years so that Jerusalem would not be destroyed.

7. Abba Sikra, head of the zealots, was son of the sister of Yohanan b. Zakkai. Yohanan asked him how long he was going to starve the people to death. The nephew said he could do nothing about it. Yohanan said, "Devise some plan for me to escape, perhaps I shall be able to save a little." Abba Sikra advised him to pretend to be sick, then to die, "let then your disciples get under your bed but no others, so that they will not notice that you are still light, since they know that a living being is lighter than a corpse." He did so and R. Eliezer went under the bier from one side, Joshua from the other. When they reached the door, some men wanted to put a lance through the bier. He said to them, "Shall they say, 'They have pierced their master'?" They wanted to give it a push, etc. He got out.

The focus of this story is not on Yohanan b. Zakkai, who takes a subordinate part. The composite of materials serves to provide a cause for the catastrophe, explaining who brought the Romans down on the Jews. Our document's story does not answer that question. The Bavli's story further stresses the zealots' destruction of the stores of food and drink and fuel, then proceeds to the further story of Martha, yielding the homily on Deut. 28:5; then turns to Sadoq. Yohanan is introduced only by making him an uncle of the head of the zealots, who form the principal actor in this version. The initiatives all belong to Abba Sikra, who tells Yohanan what to do. The disciples or Abba Sikra ("he") have the wit to get Yohanan out safely. As we shall see in a moment, Yohanan does nothing to impress Vespasian, and gets little enough from him. In a word, the Bavli's version of events does not accomplish what our document's story does, which is to place the sage into the balance as the opposite and equal of the emperor and Israel's principal actor and active intellect. I refer the reader to the text given above. I review only the most important component of the story in the version of b. Git.:

8. When he reached the Romans, he said, "Peace to you O king..." Vespasian: Your life is forfeit on two counts, first, I am not a king, and you call me one, and, second, if I am a king, why did you not come until now?" Yohanan: You are a king + Is. 11:34. But Yohanan had no answer to the other question.
9. A messenger from Rome brought word that he had been made king. Vespasian could not put on his boot, or take off the one already on his foot, because his foot had swelled with pride. Yohanan explained why and solved the problem.
10. "You can make a request of me." "Give me Yavneh and its sages, the chain of Gamaliel, and physicians to heal Sadoq."

The counterpart in The Fathers According to Rabbi Nathan is at K-T, above. With the reader's indulgence, I repeat the most important language:

K. They opened the ark and he stood before him.
L. He said to him, "Are you Rabban Yohanan ben Zakkai? Indicate what I should give you."
M. He said to him, "I ask from you only Yavneh, to which I shall go, and where I shall teach my disciples, establish prayer [Goldin: a prayer house], and carry out all of the religious duties."
N. He said to him, "Go and do whatever you want."
O. He said to him, "Would you mind if I said something to you."

P. He said to him, "Go ahead."]

Q. He said to him, "Lo, you are going to be made sovereign."

R. He said to him, "How do you know?

S. He said to him, "It is a tradition of ours that the house of the sanctuary will be given over not into the power of a commoner but of a king, for it is said, And he shall cut down the thickets of the forest with iron, and Lebanon [which refers to the Temple] shall fall by a mighty one (Is. 10:34)."

T. T. People say that not a day, two or three passed before a delegation came to him from his city indicating that the [former[Caesar had died and they had voted for him to ascend the throne.

The differences between the two stories are self-evident. The main point of difference from our perspective is that the version of The Fathers According to Rabbi Nathan serves the larger polemic of the document in favor of the supernatural standing and perception of the sage. The proposition yielded then is this: through knowledge of the Torah the sage leads Israel to the age to come, when Israel will supplant Rome. The leadership of zealots on the battlefield led to the destruction of the Temple, the senseless destruction of the food supply of Jerusalem, the calamity that had overtaken Israel. The leadership of the sages, armed with foresight and backed by God, will show the right way.

Propositional discourse defines the logic of cogent discourse and therefore of thought of all three documents — the Mishnah, Leviticus Rabbah, and The Fathers According to Rabbi Nathan. The authorships of the Mishnah and of Leviticus Rabbah set forth their propositions and prove them by appealing to the logic of syllogistic argument and the rhetoric of propositional presentation — especially that of Listenwissenschaft. That same logic in a different idiom characterized philosophical writing in the Greco-Roman, therefore also, Christian Western and Muslim Middle Eastern, intellectual worlds. And it would yield that subdivision of philosophy, natural philosophy, that in later times would yield science, beginning on the foundations of natural history.

We may hardly find surprising, therefore, the utilization of the same modes of thought and argument in the medieval Judaic philosophical tradition, exemplified, for example, by Maimonides, the paradigm of the mind of Judaism framed in the philosophical mode. Commenting on the Mishnah and then creating a restatement of the law in the manner of the Mishnah, that is, through topical sequences of propositions arrayed in logical order, Maimonides rehearsed the mind of Judaism as the Mishnah and certain other authorships would have had it. At the same time he rendered obsolete the dialectical argument of the Bavli, with its quite different mode of thought; conclusions reached, minds might move on to other matters, so he argued. The one principle of logic omitted in the repertoire of thought of Maimonides and his colleagues in philosophy was the one of fixed association, and that is the fact, even though the philosophers did resort, as needed, to the form of commentary in the expression of their propositions and arguments. But by the time of the medieval philosophers, the competing mixed mode of logic — middle-range argument, the philosophical, joined in large-scale composition of fixed association — had won the day, and the mind of Judaism joined the two logics in such a way as to close the door before a purely philosophical logic of thought and composition. But once more I have moved ahead of my argument. Let us conclude with the simple fact established by this chapter concerning the characteristic logic of important documents of the Judaism of the dual Torah.

It is that propositions lucidly stated (even though implicitly), rigorously argued, logically demonstrated formed the wherewithal of mind, the method and material of thought. In so stating, of course, we do not neglect that other logic of propositional discourse, the teleological, realized in narrative, for a different kind of philosopher later on, the one interested in the metaphysical propositions conveyed by the Qabbalah, would resort to the connections between two discrete sentences, that is to say, facts, as these are established by narrative ("begat," for example) in order to set forth propositions and draw conclusions. If the reader presently forms the impression that the mind of Judaism in the formative age exhibited an affinity with propositional thought, what now comes to the fore will surely reinforce that impression. We turn to survey that remarkable mode of discourse that establishes not one proposition but two, one at the surface, another underneath. Metapropositional discourse, of a still more characteristically-philosophical mode than the propositional discourse we have now surveyed, imparts to the mind of Judaism a still more philosophical character than that just now revealed. And the power of propositional and metapropositional argument as displayed by the formative intellects of the Judaism of the dual Torah will so impress us as to make still more puzzling the ultimate failure of philosophical logic to predominate in Judaism, as it did in Christianity, and so lead to science in Judaism, as much as in Christianity. But there is a solution to that puzzle.

CHAPTER FIVE

METAPROPOSITIONAL DISCOURSE

Propositional discourse involves setting forth facts to prove a point, such as the authorship of the Mishnah accomplished, or laying out facts to point to a conclusion, as in the case of narrative. The sort of discourse characterizes philosophy, including of course natural philosophy. Metapropositional discourse proves the unity of diverse cases by imposing a single program of analytical questions — hence "methodical-analytical" — upon a virtually unlimited range of problems. This demonstration of the proposition, within the deep structure of argument, that all things fit into a single pattern, is accomplished through sorting out many and diverse cases and the discourse repeatedly invokes a fixed set of questions. And that kind of inquiry marks science, natural and social, as we know it today. It is the supreme effort to put two and two together and therefore to explain four, or, stated more abstractly, to find, in the language of Robin Horton, "unity underlying apparent diversity...simplicity underlying apparent complexity,...order underlying apparent disorder...regularity underlying apparent anomaly."[1]

I call this classification of logic in discourse metapropositional because the effect is to present two propositions, one
immediate and at the surface, the other within the subterranean layers
of thought, with the latter the more encompassing of the two, of
course. The former — propositions concerning the case at hand, —
may derive from familiar modes of argument, making connections
between two facts and drawing a conclusion from them. Or the superficial discourse may present what appears to be merely a simple assertion of fact, with no further conclusion to be drawn or even in-
tended. But the latter — the metapropositional level — always sets
forth a fundamental proposition and proves it. For this higher level of
discourse manages time and again to make a single point even while
examining many points, and it is that capacity to conduct discourse at
two levels, the one near at hand, the other at the level of recurrent polemic, that I find remarkable. Metapropositional discourse does not
repeat itself; there is no recourse to only one proposition in every instance. But the propositions indeed prove few, and, as we survey the
canonical writings, we are impressed at the limited program of
thought encompassed by this mode of discourse: the propositions are
few, but they recur everywhere. That is why the upshot is to prove the
unities of diverse things, and to do so in such a way that, time and

---

[1] Robin Horton, "African Traditional Thought and Western Science," *Africa* 1967,
37:50-71, 155-187. William Scott Green kindly drew my attention to the stimulating
thought of Horton. I read with much appreciation also the important critique of
Hans H. Penner, "Rationality and Religion: Problems in the Comparison of Modes of
Thought," *Journal of the American Academy of Religion* 1986, 54:645-672. See
*also Modes of Thought. Essays on Thinking in Western and Non-Western Socie-
ties*, ed. by Robin Horton and Ruth Finnegan (London, 1973: Faber & Faber),
where a number of important essays on Horton's article, as well as Horton's response, are collected. The issue on which Horton's essay focuses, the points in
common and the contrasts between African traditional thought and Western science,
is not pertinent here. I make no judgment on the matter, since my treatment of science ends in the period in which science still formed part of philosophy, and that is
long before the advent of experimental science and the development of science as
an autonomous realm of intellect.

again, we find ourselves able to articulate the proposition that is demonstrated through recurrent proofs of little things.

Metapropositional discourse of course forms a subdivision of propositional discourse. What distinguishes this species from its genus is not only that in these cases, the compositors make two points, one on the surface, another underneath. It also is that this mode of thought, seeking unity in diversity in a highly particular way, affects a broad range of documents; it is an instance of that process that, in the aggregate, defines traits indicative not of particular documents but of large sectors of the canon as a whole. Indeed, the intellectually highly-structured character of the Mishnah, with its systematic and orderly exposition of the extension or restriction of rules, its rigorous exercise in comparison and contrast, sets the style and defines the task for later authorships, to the end of the formation of the canon in late antiquity. Not only so, but the mind trained in seeking unity in diversity, and unity susceptible of statement in proposition, works systematically through an amazingly broad program of topical inquiry and repeatedly produces that single, besought result. Out of this kind of mind, capable of making connections among wildly diverse data, science can have arisen, so far as science seeks connections and draws conclusions to explain connections. But in so stating, I have once more moved too far ahead of my argument. What of the propositional character of metapropositional discourse?

The propositions that are proven in each instance are in one case minor and in the other, encompassing. The minor proposition is on the surface, the rule prevailing in a detail of law. The encompassing generalization bears global consequence, that is, for example, reason along bears reliable results, and the like. Commonly, the surface-generalization forms little more than a clause of a verse followed by a phrase in amplification thereof. Yet the unit of thought may be enormous, relative to the size — number of words — of the completed units of thought in our document. Reading the cases of Scripture and transforming them into general rules suitable for restatement in, and as, the Mishnah, the authorship of Sifré to Deuteronomy, for example, accomplished an amazing fete of sheer brilliance: holding many things together within a single theoretical framework. What is critical in holding together discourse in these items therefore is the imposition of a fixed analytical method, rather than the search for a generalization and its demonstration or proof. These items are topically discrete but time and again present the application of a fixed analytical system or structure or produce, in an episodic instance, a recurrent proposition of an analytical character (e.g., extension or restriction of a rule, demonstration that solely through Scripture are firm conclusions to be established).

One recurring exercise, which fills up much of the discussion of the legal passages of Deuteronomy in Sifré to Deuteronomy, for example, systematically proposes to generalize the case-discourse of the book of Deuteronomy and to reframe the case into the example of a law. The "if a person does such and so," or the details of a case as spelled out in Scripture will be subjected to a sustained exercise of generalization. In this exercise we do two things. Either — in the process of generalization — we restrict the rule, or we extend it. If Scripture contains a detail, such as the statement of a case always demands, we ask whether that detail restricts the rule to a kind of case defined by the detail, or whether that detail represents a more general category of cases and is to be subjected, therefore, to generalization. (In the unfortunate word-choice of contemporary philosophy, the fixed analytical method at hand investigates issues of generalizability.) Here is an example of many instances in which the authorship of a sustained discourse proposes to turn a case into a law.

Sifré to Deuteronomy CLXVI:I

1. A. "[You shall also give him] the first fruits of your new grain and wine and oil, [and the first shearing of your sheep. For the Lord your God has chosen him and his descendants, out of all your tribes, to be in attendance for service in the name of the Lord for all time]" (Dt. 18:1-6):

   B. This teaches that offerings are taken up for the priestly rations only from produce of the finest quality.
   The point applies to more than the case at hand. At issue is whether we extend or restrict the applicability of the rule. Here we restrict it.

2. A. Just as we find that as to two varieties of produce of fruit-bearing trees, priestly rations are not taken from the one to provide the requisite gift for

the other as well,

B.   so in the case of two varieties of produce of grain and vegetables, priestly rations are not taken from the one to provide the requisite gift for the other as well.

No. 2 is parachuted down and has no bearing upon anything in the cited verse. But the importance is to derive a general rule, as stated at B, which applies to a broad variety of categories of priestly gifts, just as at No. 1.

CLXVI:II

1.   A.   "...the first shearing of your sheep:"
     B.   not the fleece the falls off when the sheep is dipped.
2.   A.   "...the first shearing of your sheep:"
     B.   excluding a sheep that suffers from a potentially fatal ailment.
3.   A.   "...the first shearing of your sheep:"
     B.   whether in the land or abroad.

No. 1 is particular to our verse, Nos. 2, 3 are general rules invoked case by case. These items are not coherent, one by one, and the three sentences in no way state a single proposition, explicit or otherwise. And yet the exercise of analysis is uniform — I could give many dozens of cases in which precisely the same distinctions are made — and the purpose is clear. It is to impose upon the case a set of generalizing issues, which yield either restrictive or expansive definitions. This is a fine instance of what I mean by attaining cogent discourse — linking one sentence to another — through an established methodical analysis of one sort of another.

CLXVI:IV

1.   A.   "You shall also give him:"
     B.   This indicates that there should be sufficient fleece to constitute a gift.
     C.   On this basis sages have ruled:
     D.   How much does one give to the priest?
     E.   Five selas' weight in Judah, equivalent to ten in Galilee, bleached but not spun,
     F.   sufficient to make a small garment from it,
     G.   as it is said, "You shall also give him:"
     H.   This indicates that there should be sufficient fleece to constitute a gift.

The same pattern recurs as before, and the interest is in an autonomous program. This represents a different kind of methodical analysis. The framer wishes to relate a verse of Scripture to a rule in the Mishnah and so asks how C-F are founded on Scripture. G-H go over the ground of A-B. The work of restriction or expansion of the rule is now implicit, of course.

Another recurrent proposition, important in Sifra and the two Sifrés, addresses the question of whether reason unguided by Scripture attains reliable results and shows that it cannot. Indeed, the polemic is so powerful and so ubiquitous that one wonders who, in the third and fourth centuries, maintained otherwise. Sifra's authorship presents us with a moving, or dialectical, argument, in which we progress from point to point, or from one thing to its opposite, in a search not only for harmonies but for the fundamental unity of reason and revelation. Reason may be represented by a hypothesis which stands on its own, without resort to the revealed proof of the written Torah, Scripture; or reason may be identified with a rule of the Mishnah, in the language of the Mishnah (or the Tosefta). In either case, the authorship of the Sifra wants to know whether or not a given rule is a matter of (mere) logic and invariably proves that it is not. The mode of thought is absolutely uniform throughout, the quest and purpose always yielding a single proposition: never reason alone, always reason informed and also restricted by Scripture. And that defines the metaproposition of this highly structured patterned mode of thought. In Sifra, for one instance, we find the following.

Sifra Parashat Negaim Pereq 1

A.   When there will be (Lev. 12:2) —
B.   From the [time at which this law is] proclaimed [namely, Sinai] onward.
C.   And is it not logical?
D.   It [Scripture] has declared unclean with reference to Zabim and has declared unclean with reference to plagues.
E.   Just as in the case of Zabim, it declared clear [such appearances of uncleanness as occurred] before the pronouncement [of the Torah], so in reference to plagues, it declared clear [such appearances of uncleanness as occurred] on them before the pronouncement.

N1:2

F.   It [moreover] is an argument a fortiori:
     If in the case of Zabim [Leviticus Chapter 15], whose uncleanness and un-
     cleanness may be determined by anyone, it [Scripture] has declared free be-
     fore the declaration, plagues, the uncleanness or cleanness of which may be
     declared only by a priest, is it not logical that it should declare them clear be-
     fore the declaration?

G.   No. If you have so stated concerning Zabim, whom it [Scripture] did not de-
     clare unclean when [the flux is] accidental, will you say so concerning plague,
     which is declared unclean [even when the uncleanness is] accidental?

H.   Since is declared unclean [even when the uncleanness is] accidental, will it
     declare them clear before the pronouncement [of the Scriptural law]?

I.   Therefore Scripture says, When it well be, meaning, from the pronouncement
     [at Sinai] and onward.

N1:3

At stake is not only the proposition that the laws at hand, those declared at Lev. 13-14, apply only from the giving of the Torah and onward. It is also the further proposition that through reason alone we
could not have reached that conclusion, since contrary arguments
can have been proposed. Accordingly, we see a double proposition,
the one immediate, the other at the deep structure of thought.

A second recurrent interest, which yields the effect of showing the fundamental unity of many things in one thing, will take the
case to which Scripture refers and ask whether the case exemplifies a
rule that applies to many cases, or whether the details of Scripture's
case constitute limitations upon a rule. The rule then applies only to
details exactly like those at hand. In the following, we ask whether any
priest may inspect the skin disease at hand, or whether only Aaron in
particular, who is mentioned by name, may do so. Since the proposition that only Aaron may inspect the cases of the skin disease is ab-
surd, it is the exercise itself which is the centerpiece of interest.

A.   And he will be brought to Aaron [the priest or to one of his sons the priests]
     (Lev. 13:2).

B.   I know only about Aaron himself.

C.   How do we know to include another priest?

D.   Scripture says, The priest (Lev. 13:2).

E.   How do we know to include [as suitable examining priests] those [priests who are] injured?

F.   Scripture says, Among his sons (Lev. 13:2).

G.   Then perhaps should I also include profaned [disqualified priests, HLLYM]?

H.   Scripture says, The priests (Lev. 13:2) — the disqualified priests are excluded.

I.   And how do we know to include any Israelite [qualified to examine the plague]?

J.   Scripture says, Or to one.

       N1:8

K.   If our end is to include every Israelite, why does Scripture say, Or to one of his sons the priests?

L.   But to teach that the actual declaration of uncleanness or cleanness is only by a priest.

M.   How so?

N.   A sage who is an Israelite examines the plagues and says to the priest, even though he is an idiot, Say, Unclean, and he says, Unclean. Say, Clean, and he says, Clean [M. Neg. 3:1].

O.   Another matter:

P.   Why does Scripture say, Or to one of his sons the priests (Lev. 13:2)

Q.   Since it is said, In accord with their instructions will be every dispute and every plague (Deut. 21:5), controversies are linked to plagues. Just as plagues must be decided by day, so controversies must be judged by day.

N1:9

R.   Just as controversies may not be settled by relatives, so plagues may not be examined relatives [M. Neg. 2:5].

S.   If [we should now attempt to continue]: Just as controversies must be with three [judges] so plagues must be examined by three [priests] — it is an argument a fortiori.

T.   If his property [dispute] is settled by a decision of three judges, should his body not be examined by three?

U.   Scripture says, Or to one of his sons the priests (Lev. 13:2).

V.   This teaches that a single priest examines the plagues.

       N1:10

What is interesting in the protracted and moving discussion at hand is that the subject changes as we proceed, but the basic program of inquiry remains constant. This moving, or dialectical, argument forms the definitive mode of discourse of the Bavli, as we shall see presently, and characterizes the mind of Judaism at its most formidable and rigorous.

     Yet a third subterranean proposition, amply displayed in Sifra, is that the laws of the Mishnah, which are generally presented without proof-texts, in fact relate directly to, and rest upon, explicit teachings of Scripture. That metapropositional position comes to expression in numerous ways. One of course has already come before us: proof that Scripture, not reason alone, is needed to sustain the law, very often encompasses a proposition stated by the Mishnah, without an accompanying citation of Scripture. The net effect is to make the implicit point that the rule of the Mishnah requires a proof-text of Scripture; since the authorship of the Mishnah omitted it, the writers of Sifra (and other documents, as we shall presently see) persistently add it. Here is a representative case.

Parashat Negaim Pereq 2

A. And the priest shall see the diseased spot (Lev. 13:3) —
   His eyes should be upon it when he sees it.

B. [And the priest shall examine the diseased spot] on the skin [of the flesh] (Lev. 13:3) —

C. On skin of the flesh of an intermediate [color].

D. On the skin of the flesh (Lev. 13:3) —

E. That he should see all of the flesh with it in one glance.

F. R. Yose b. R. Judah says, Why does Scripture say, On the skin of the flesh (Lev. 13:3)?

G. That all which is outside it be near the skin of the flesh and suitable for spreading.

H. For if it was near the head or the beard or the boil or the burning or the blister which are festering, it is not unclean [M. Neg. 2:12].

N2:1

A. [And if the hair (in the diseased spot [plague]) [has turned white and the disease appears to be deeper than the skin of his body, it is a leprous disease (Lev. 13:3)].

B. And hair (Lev. 13:3) — the smallest quantity of hair is two hairs.

C. On the plague —

D. to include what is inside it and lies outside it,

E. excluding that which is outside it and lying inside it.

F. In the diseased spot has turned white (Lev. 13:3) —

G. not that which was there before.

H. On this basis they have said:

I. If the bright spot preceded the white hair, it is unclean, and if white hair preceded the bright spot, it is clean, and if there is doubt [as to which came first], it is unclean.

J. R. Joshua says, It is doubtful [M. Neg. 4:11].

N2:2

A.   And [if] the hair in the diseased spot has turned white (Lev. 13:3).

B.   On this basis have they said:

C.   Two hairs, their root is black and their head is white — it is clean.

D.   Their root is white and their head is black — unclean.

E.   And how much must be in the whiteness?

F.   R. Meir says, Any amount at all [M. Neg. 4:4].

G.   And sages say, About [the length of] the hair.

H.   R. Meir says, That people should not imagine that they are judged by ignoramuses.

   But [if] the tip (HWD) of the hair is white, it is unclean. But [if] it is not (a) white (hair), it is clean [M. Neg. 2:2].

N2:3 (b. Nid. 52b)

A.   And the disease appears to be deeper than the skin of his body — it is a leprous disease (Lev. 13:3) —

B.   Why does Scripture say this?

C.   Because it is said, [When the priest has examined him], he shall declare him unclean, he shall not shut him up (Lev. 13:11) —

D.   We learned that:

E.   they do not shut up one who has been certified unclean [M. Neg. 3:1].

N2:6

A.   How do we know that:

   they do not certify as unclean one who has been shut up, and they do not shut up one who has been shut up, and they do not certify one who has been certified? [M. Neg. 3:1]?

B.   Scripture says, And he will not shut him up, because he is unclean (Lev. 13:11).

C.   Whoever is called unclean is not subject on its [another spot's] account.

   N2:7

In the continuation, we develop two metapropositions at once, first, the necessity of a proof-text, not logic alone, second, the requirement of a proof-text for a Mishnaic teaching:

A.   Might one say, One should not say, Lo, you are shut up on account of this one and certified on account of this one, certified on account of this one and shut up on account of this one, and certified on account of this and on account of that?

B.   Scripture says, It is a diseased spot (Lev. 13:3). And he will see it (Lev. 13:3).

C.   It is a leprous disease and he will see it (Lev. 13:3) —

D.   1.   all at once.

2.   That

if it was on the tip of his nose, protruding this way and that, on the tip of his finger, protruding this way and that, he is not unclean [M. Neg. 2:12].

N2:8

E.   On this basis they have said:

Twenty four tips of limbs are in man which are not made unclean because of quick flesh:

the tips of the fingers of the hands, and toes of the feet, and the tips of the ears, and the tip of the nose, and the tip of the penis, and the tips of the breasts in the woman.

R. Judah says, Also of the man.

R. Eleazar says, The wens and the warts and warts are not made unclean because of quick flesh [M. Neg. 6:7].

N2:9

A.   And he will declare him unclean (Lev. 13:3).

B.   Him [whose tokens of uncleanness he has seen] does he declare unclean, and he does not declare unclean him who uproots the tokens of uncleanness from the midst of his diseased spot before he came to the priest.

C.   Said R. Aqiba, I asked R. Ishmael and R. Joshua while they were going to Nidbat:

D.   [If he does so] during his quarantine, what is the law?

E.   They said to him, We have not heard, but we have heard, Before he came to the priest, he is clean; after he is certified unclean, he is unclean.

F.   I began to bring proofs for them.

G.   On what account is he clean if he does so before he came to the priest? Is it not because the priest has not actually seen the tokens of uncleanness?

H.   So if this happens while he is shut up, he is clean until the priest will declare him unclean.

I.   Another version:

J.   If he is standing before the priest —

K.   it is all the same whether he is standing before the priest or whether he is standing during his quarantine, he is clean until the priest will declare him unclean.

L.   They said to him, Well have you spoken.

M.   When is his purification?

N.   R. Eliezer says, When another diseased spot will appear in him, and he will be declared clean on its account.

O.   And sages say, Until it breaks forth over his entire body, or until his [original] bright spot will diminish to less than the size of a split bean [M. Neg. 7:4, T. 3:4].

N2:10

It remains to call attention to the obvious trait of mind throughout, which is the highly imaginative and speculative, broad-ranging character of intellect exhibited by this authorship (and the many that are like it). Stimulated by a recurring question, guided by an absolutely sure inquiry, our authorship knows no limits in the speculation represented by "might one thing," or "may we suppose?" Quite to the contrary, the metapropositional mode of thought seeking the unity of diversity, the explanation of connection between (superficially) unconnected things, precipitates a virtually unlimited process of the testing of hypotheses, much as does science in its explanation of connection and search for hypothesis by way of explanation. Nor should the reader imagine that Sifra stands by itself in its powerful exercise of imagination and disciplined speculation. The contrary is the case.

Now that we have seen the repertoire of propositions we may expect to locate within the deep structure of discourse, let us address a sizable segment of a complete chapter, a sustained passage of yet other important document, Sifré to Numbers, and ask whether, within its masses of detail, we may pick out those propositions that make of many things one thing, turning much detail into a few fundamental and well-proven truths. We take up the opening pisqa of Sifré to Numbers, and I insert my comments as we proceed:

Sifré to Numbers I:I.1

A.   "The Lord said to Moses, 'Command the people of Israel that they put out of the camp [every leper and every one having a discharge, and every one that is unclean through contact with the dead]'" (Num. 5:1-2).

B.   For what purpose is this passage presented?

C.   Because it is said, "But the man who is unclean and does not cleanse himself, [that person shall be cut off from the midst of the assembly, since he has defiled the sanctuary of the Lord, because the water for impurity has not been thrown upon him, he is unclean]" (Num. 19:20).

D.   Consequently, we are informed of the penalty [for contaminating the sanctuary]. But where are we informed of the admonition not to do so?

E.   Scripture accordingly states, "Command the people of Israel that they put out of the camp every leper and every one having a discharge, and every one that is unclean through contact with the dead" (Num. 5:1-2).

F.   Lo, here is an admonition that unclean persons not come into the sanctuary ["out of the camp"] in a state of uncleanness. [Consequently, the entire transaction — admonition, then penalty — is laid forth.]

The premise is that wherever there is a rule, there also is an admonition. So B-D. A further premise is that Moses did not repeat himself; there was a clear purpose for each statement that he made in the Torah.

I:II.1

A. "Command" (Num. 5:2):

B. The commandment at hand is meant both to be put into effect immediately and also to apply for generations to come.

C. You maintain that the commandment at hand is meant both to be put into effect immediately and also to apply for generations to come.

D. But perhaps the commandment is meant to apply only after a time [but not right away, at the moment at which it was given].

E. [We shall now prove that the formulation encompasses both generations to come and also the generation to whom the commandment is entrusted.] Scripture states, "The Lord said to Moses, 'Command the people of Israel that they put out [of the camp every leper and every one having a discharge, and every one that is unclean through contact with the dead. You shall put out both male and female, putting them outside the camp, that they may not defile their camp, in the midst of which I dwell.'] And the people of Israel did so and drove them outside the camp, as the Lord said to Moses, so the people of Israel did" (Num. 5:1-4). [The verse itself makes explicit the fact that the requirement applied forthwith, not only later on.]

F. Lo, we have learned that the commandment at hand is meant to be put into effect immediately.

G. How then do we derive from Scripture the fact that it applies also for generations to come? [We shall now show that the same word used here, command, pertains to generations to come and not only to the generation at hand.]

H. Scripture states, "Command the children of Israel to bring you pure oil from beaten olives [for the .lamp, that a light may be kept burning continually outside the veil of the testimony in the tent of meeting, Aaron shall keep it in order from evening to morning before the Lord continually; it shall be a statute for ever throughout your generations]" (Lev. 24:2).

I. Lo, we here derive evidence that the commandment at hand is meant both to be put into effect immediately and also to apply for generations to come, [based on the framing of the present commandment].

J. How, then, do we drive evidence that all of the commandments that are contained in the Torah [apply in the same way]? [We wish now to prove that the language, command, always bears the meaning imputed to it here.]

K.   R. Ishmael maintained, "Since the bulk of the commandments stated in the To-
      rah are presented without further amplification, while in the case of one of
      them [namely, the one at hand], Scripture has given explicit details, that com-
      mandment [that has been singled out] is meant both to be put into effect im-
      mediately and also to apply for generations to come. Accordingly, I apply to all
      of the other commandments in the Torah the same detail, so that in all cases
      the commandment is meant both to be put into effect immediately and also to
      apply for generations to come."

In this moving, or dialectical, discourse, once more we notice an issue upon which we stumbled, also, in Sifra, namely, whether
or not a commandment applied immediately or only at some later
point. Or whether it applied only to the generation to which it was
given, namely, that of Sinai, so C. F solves that problem, and G pursues it. J then tests the result as a further hypothesis: if this, then that,
if that, then always that? The reader can be certain that this question
and mode of answering it, producing not only a ruling for the case at
hand, but a law characteristic of the structure of the system as a
whole, recurs time and again, throughout both Sifrés. Now we gain a
fine insight into the working of metapropositional thought and see the
implicit, large-scale propositions that are at stake. We revert to a systematic and propositional argument:

I.III.1
A.   R. Judah b. Beterah says, "The effect of a commandment stated in any context
      serves only [1] to lend encouragement.
B.   "For it is said, 'But command Joshua and encourage and strengthen him'
      (Deut. 3:28).
C.   "Accordingly, we derive the lesson that strength is granted only to the strong,
      and encouragement only to the stout of heart."
D.   R. Simeon b. Yohai says, "The purpose of a commandment in any context is
      only [2] to deal with the expenditure of money, as it is said, 'Command the
      children of Israel to bring you pure oil from beaten olives for the .lamp, that a
      light may be kept burning continually outside the veil of the testimony in the
      tent of meeting, Aaron shall keep it in order from evening to morning before
      the Lord continually; it shall be a statute for ever throughout your genera-
      tions' (Lev. 24:2). 'Command the people of Israel that they put out of the
      camp every leper and every one having a discharge, and every one that is un-
      clean through contact with the dead' (Num. 5:1-2). 'Command the children
      of Israel that they give to the Levites from the inheritance of their possession

cities to dwell in, and you shall give to the Levites pasture lands round about the cities' (Num. 35:2). 'Command the people of Israel and say to them, "My offering, my food for my offerings by fire, my pleasing odor you shall take heed to offer to me in its due season"' (Num. 28:2). Lo, we see in all these cases that the purpose of a commandment is solely to bring about the expenditure of money.

E.   "There is one exception, and what is that? It is this verse: 'Command the people of Israel and say to them, "When you enter the land of Canaan, this is the land that shall fall to you for an inheritance, the land of Canaan in its full extent"' (Num. 34:2).

F.   "You must give encouragement to them in the matter of the correct division of the land."

G.   And Rabbi [Judah the Patriarch] says, "The use of the word, 'commandment' in all passages serves only for the purpose of [3] imparting an admonition [not to do a given action], along the lines of the following: 'And the Lord God commanded the man, saying, "You may freely eat of every tree of the garden, but of the tree of the knowledge of good and evil you shall not eat"' (Gen. 2:16)."

Here we have a propositional discourse, with the proposed propositions at C, resting on B; then at D, with enormous proof deriving from a variety of cases (hence, unity in diversity at a merely-propositional level). Again, at G we have an effort to generalize a case into a proposition. The net effect is to move from facts to generalizations at that middle range to which I referred at the outset.

I:IV.1

A.   "[The Lord said to Moses, 'Command the people of Israel that] they put out of the camp [every leper and every one having a discharge, and every one that is unclean through contact with the dead']" (Num. 5:1-2).

B.   Is it from the [innermost] camp, of the Presence of God, or should I infer that it is only from the camp of the Levites?

C.   Scripture states, "...they put out them of the camp." [The sense is that they are to be put outside of the camp of the Presence.]

D.   Now even if Scripture had not made the matter explicit, I could have proposed the same proposition on the basis of reasoning [that they should be put outside of the camp of the Presence]:

E.   If unclean people are driven out of the camp that contains the ark, which is of lesser sanctity, all the more so should they be driven out of the camp of the Presence of God, which is of greater sanctuary.

F.   But if you had proposed reasoning on that basis, you would have found yourself in the position of imposing a penalty merely on the basis of reason [and not on the basis of an explicit statement of Scripture, and one does not impose a penalty merely on the basis of reason].

G.   Then is why it is stated: "...they put out of the camp"?

H.   Making that matter explicit in Scripture serves to teach you that penalties are not to be imposed merely on the basis of logic [but require explicit specification in Scripture]. [That is, Scripture made a point that reason could have reached, but Scripture made the matter explicit so as to articulate a penalty applicable for violating the rule.]

I.   [Rejecting that principle,] Rabbi says, "It is not necessary for Scripture to make the matter explicit, since it is a matter of an argument a fortiori :

J.   "If the unclean people are driven out of the camp that contains the ark, which is of lesser sanctity, all the more so should they be driven out of the camp of the Presence of God, which is of greater sanctity.

K.   "Then is why it is stated: '...they put out of the camp every leper and every one having a discharge, and every one that is unclean through contact with the dead'?

L.   "[By specifying that all three are put out of the camp,] Scripture thereby served to assign to them levels or gradations [of uncleanness, with diverse rules affecting those levels, as will now be spelled out. Since we know that that rule applies to the ostracism of the leper, the specification that the others also are to be put out of the camp indicates that a singular rule applies to each of the category. If one rule applied in common, then the specification with respect to the leper alone would have sufficed to indicate the rule for all others.]"

M.   [We review the distinctions among several gradations of uncleanness affecting human beings, inclusive of the three at hand: the leper, the one having a discharge, and the one unclean through contact with the dead.] "The Lord said to Moses, 'Command the people of Israel that they put out of the camp every leper and every one having a discharge, and every one that is unclean through contact with the dead'" (Num. 5:1-2).

N.   Shall I then draw the conclusion that all three of those listed [the leper, the one affected by a discharge, the one unclean with corpse-uncleanness] are to remain in the same locale [in relationship to the Temple]?

O.   With respect to the leper, Scripture states explicit, "He shall dwell by himself; outside of the camp shall be his dwelling" (Lev. 13:46).

P.   Now the leper fell into the same category as the others, and he has been singled out from the general category, thereby serving to impose a single rule on the category from which he has been singled out.

Q.   [And this is the rule applicable to the leper and hence to the others from among whom he has been singled out:] Just as in the case of the leper, who is subject to a most severe form of uncleanness, and who also is subjected to a more severe rule governing ostracism than that applying to his fellow, so all who are subject to a more severe form of uncleanness likewise are subject to a more severe rule of ostracism than that applying to his fellow.

R. On this basis sages listed distinctions that apply to those that are unclean [since a different rule applies to each of them, in descending order of severity, as is now spelled out]:

S. To any object that one affected by a flux imparts uncleanness, a leper imparts uncleanness. A leper is subject to a more severe rule, however, in that a leper imparts uncleanness through an act of sexual relations.

T. To any object that one unclean with corpse-uncleanness imparts uncleanness, one affected by a flux imparts uncleanness. But a more severe rule affects one affected by a flux, in that he imparts uncleanness to an object located far beneath a rock in the deep [imparting uncleanness to that deeply-buried object merely by the application of the pressure of his weight, while one unclean with corpse-uncleanness does not impart uncleanness merely by pressure of his weight alone].

U. To any object that one unclean by reason of waiting for sunset after immersion imparts uncleanness one unclean by corpse-uncleanness imparts uncleanness. A more severe rule applies to one unclean by corpse-uncleanness, for he imparts uncleanness to a human being [which is not the case of one who is unclean by reason of waiting for sunset after his immersion].

V. What is made unfit by one who has not yet completed his rites of atonement following uncleanness and purification is made unfit by one who awaits for sunset to complete his process of purification. A more strict rule applies to one awaiting sunset for the completion of his rite of purification, for he imparts unfitness to food designated for priestly rations [while the one who has completed his rites of purification but not yet offered the atonement-sacrifice on account of his uncleanness does not impart unfitness to priestly rations that he may touch].

I need hardly remind the reader of the metaproposition before us: could I have reached the proposed conclusion other than by appeal to Scripture, so D? F explains why not. G-H draw a conclusion for the case at hand, yielding an implicit metaproposition pointing toward the inner structure of the system as a whole. The work from M onward performs that comparison of species, comparing and contrasting them all in an effort to define the genus, that the framers of the Mishnah did so well. I cannot imagine a more stunning proof of the power of taxonomic thinking both to sort out masses of otherwise senseless detail and also to point to the few unities that emerge from unlimited diversities. I need point to no more ample evidence of the speculative and imaginative character of the mind of Judaism than the work of the intellect behind this architectonically perfect passage. A further survey of the same document, even of the chapter at hand, can yield only more examples of the same kind of rigorous and patterned thinking, the presence of a severely limited repertoire of logics, to which I alluded in Chapter Three. For the sake of brevity, however, I give only one further abstract. The next item pursues the perennial problem of restricting or extending the applicability of the law. The interest, obviously, is to extend it.

I:VII.1

A.   "[The Lord said to Moses, 'Command the people of Israel that they put out of the camp every leper and every one having a discharge, and every one that is unclean through contact with the dead.] You shall put out both male and female, putting them outside the camp, that they may not defile their camp, in the midst of which I dwell'" (Num. 5:1-4)

B.   I know, on the basis of the stated verse, that the law applies only to male and female [persons who are suffering from the specified forms of cultic uncleanness]. How do I know that the law pertains also to one lacking clearly defined sexual traits or to one possessed of the sexual traits of both genders?

C.   Scripture states, "...putting them outside the camp." [This is taken to constitute an encompassing formulation, extending beyond the male and female of the prior clause.]

D.   I know, on the basis of the stated verse, that the law applies only to those who can be sent forth. How do I know that the law pertains also to those who cannot be sent forth?

E.   Scripture states, "...putting them outside the camp." [This is taken to constitute an encompassing formulation, as before.]

F.   I know on the basis of the stated verse that the law applies only to persons. How do I know that the law pertains also to utensils?

G.   Scripture states, "...putting them outside the camp." [This is taken to constitute an encompassing formulation.]

I:VII.2.

A.   [Dealing with the same question as at 1.F,] R. Aqiba says, "'You shall put out both male and female, putting them outside the camp.' Both persons and utensils are implied."

B.   R. Ishmael says, "You may construct a logical argument, as follows:

C.   "Since man is subject to uncleanness on account of Negaim ["plagues"], and clothing [thus: utensils] are subject to uncleanness on the same count, just as man is subject to being sent forth [ostracism], likewise utensils are subject to being sent forth."

D.   No, such an argument is not valid [and hence exegesis of the actual language of Scripture, as at A, is the sole correct route]. If you have stated the rule in the case of man, who imparts uncleanness when he exerts pressure on an object used for either sitting or lying, and, on which account, he is subject to ostracism, will you say the same rule of utensils, which do not impart uncleanness when they exert pressure on an object used for sitting and lying? [Clearly there is a difference between the uncleanness brought about by a human being from that brought about by an inanimate object, and therefore the rule that applies to the one will not necessarily apply to the other. Logic by itself will not suffice, and, it must follow, the proof of a verse of Scripture alone will suffice to prove the point.]

E.   [No, that objection is not valid, because we can show that the same rule does apply to both an inanimate object and to man, namely] lo, there is the case of the stone affected with a Nega, which will prove the point. For it does not impart uncleanness when it exerts pressure on an object used for sitting or lying, but it does require ostracism [being sent forth from the camp, a rule that Scripture itself makes explicit].

F.   Therefore do not find it surprising that utensils, even though they in general do not impart uncleanness when they exert pressure on an object used for sitting or lying, are to be sent forth from the camp." [Ishmael's logical proof stands.]

Once more we have demonstrated the fallibility of reason unrestricted by revelation. The conclusion of the chapter at hand is of interest, because it shows us how, at the end, the framers of the document insert a sequence of encompassing generalizations:

I:X.2

A.   R. Yose the Galilean says, "Come and take note of how great is the power of sin. For before the people had laid hands on transgression, people afflicted with flux and lepers were not located among them, but after they had laid hands on transgression, people afflicted with flux and lepers did find a place among them.

B.   "Accordingly, we learn that these three events took place on one and the same day: [transgression, the presence of those afflicted with flux, the development of leprosy among the people].

Here is another syllogism, this time in the form of narrative. The events took place on one day, which proves the proposition that

sin is powerful. The sequence, first this, then that, explains why that
— the teleological logic of propositional discourse we identified in so
much more subtle terms earlier. The same mode of argument proceeds in the following.

I:X.3
A. R. Simeon b. Yohai says, "Come and take note of how great is the power of sin.
    For before the people had laid hands on transgression, what is stated in their
    regard?
B. "'Now the appearance of the glory of the Lord was like a devouring fire on the
    top of the mountain in the sight of the people of Israel' (Ex. 24:17).
C. "Nonetheless, the people did not fear nor were they afraid.
D. "But once they had laid hands on transgression, what is said in their regard?
E. "'And when Aaron and all the people of Israel saw Moses, behold, the skin of
    his face shone, and they were afraid to come near him' (Ex. 34:30)."

I:XI.1
A. "[You shall put out both male and female, putting them outside the camp, that
    they may not defile their camp, in the midst of which I dwell.' And the people
    of Israel did so and drove them outside the camp, as the Lord said to Moses,]
    so the people of Israel did" (Num. 5:3-4):
B. This statement, ["...And the people of Israel did so,"] serves to recount praise
    for the Israelites, for just as Moses instructed them, so did they do.

I:XI.2
A. Scripture states, "...as the Lord said to Moses, so the people of Israel did."
B. What this teaches is that even the unclean people did not register opposition
    [but accepted the decree without complaint].

The miscellanies tacked on at the end draw a moral from the
entire discussion. First, the people did what they were told; second,
the unclean people accepted their penalty. These are further conclusions argued on the basis of the evidence at hand, propositions in a
normal sequence of an unfolding argument. I need hardly underline
the simple fact that the reader will already have noted. What holds the
whole together is not the mere sequence of verses in the cited passage
of the book of Numbers.

Rather, we have an unfolding sequence of middle-range
propositions and metapropositional discourses, each one of sizable

proportions and noteworthy cogency. To state the opposite: we do not have merely a sequence of unrelated sentences (or facts), all of them sewn onto the hem of a single set of verses of Scripture, none of them sewn to any other, on either side. That sort of fixed associative mode of sustained and cogent discourse in no way characterizes the document before us, any more than we find it in the Mishnah, Genesis Rabbah, Leviticus Rabbah, Pesiqta deRab Kahana, or other writings. For the authorships of all of those documents (and the many like them), connections derive not from an extrinsic, non-propositional source, but from an intrinsic, and therefore necessarily propositional, or metapropositional, quest. To put it plainly, the authorships of propositional or metapropositional compositions, whether small or enormous, make connections for themselves, rather than finding them ready-made in Scripture or in some other inherited text. The contrast between those authorships and the ones of the Tosefta and the two Talmuds will become clear in the next chapter.

First, however, we address both Talmuds, to find in each the same evidences of a fixed program of metapropositional discourse. That demonstration will permit us to understand the choices made by the authorships of the two Talmuds, when, presenting their massive compositions, they selected in the end not one but two large-scale constitutive logics: one, propositional, the other, fixed associative — a fixed associative and not a propositional or metapropositional mode of discourse for holding the whole together. In that way they defined the mind of Judaism, for the most of its range of power and effect, as fixed associative rather than propositional in its modes of thought: the making of connections, the drawing of conclusions. To state matters very simply, the two Talmuds present literally thousands of discrete discussions that, all together, demonstrate a few fundamental points. Metapropositional thought flourished in the making of both vast treatments of the Mishnah. In order to explain what is at stake, let me turn to the Talmud of the Land of Israel, or Yerushalmi, and explain how the authorship of that document did the same thing to many things, proved the same point at the deep structure of thousands of discrete and episodic proofs of little things. The authorship of the

Yerushalmi provided a systematic exegesis of selected passages of the Mishnah, doing pretty much a single set of operations wherever it turned. I review a taxonomy of these exegeses. What are the sorts of approaches we are apt to find? These are four:

1. Citation and gloss of the language of the Mishnah (meaning of a phrase or concrete illustration of a rule). A unit of discourse of this type will contain a direct citation of a sentence of the Mishnah. The word choices or phrasing of the Mishnah will be paraphrased or otherwise explained through what is essentially a gloss. Or the rule of the Mishnah will be explained through an example or a restatement of some kind. The premise is of course that a single mode of exegesis serves the whole of the Mishnah, and the upshot is the homogenization and harmonization of all passages of the Mishnah into a simple cogent whole.

2. Specification of the meaning of the law of the Mishnah or the reason for it. Items of this type stand very close to those of the former. What differentiates the one from the other is the absence, in the present set of units of discourse, of direct citation of the Mishnah or close and explicit reading of its language. The discussion then tends to allude to the Mishnah or to generalize, while remaining wholly within its framework. In some units of discourse scriptural proof texts are adduced in evidence of a Mishnah passage. These frequently spill over into discussion of the reason for a rule.

3. Secondary implication or application of the law of the Mishnah. Units of discourse of this catalog generalize beyond the specific rule of the Mishnah. The discussion will commonly restate the principle of the rule at hand or raise a question invited by it. Hence if the Mishnah's law settles one question, participants in this type of discourse will use that as the foundation for raising a second and consequent question. Two or more rules of the

Mishnah (or of the Mishnah and Tosefta) will be contrasted with one another and then harmonized, or two or more rulings of a specific authority will be alleged to conflict and then shown not to stand at variance with one another.

4. The matter of authorities and their views: case law. In a handful of items, concrete decisions are attached to specific laws of the Mishnah, or the harmonization or identification of the opinions of Mishnah's authorities forms the center of interest.

From this taxonomy it follows that there was a severely circumscribed repertoire of intellectual initiatives available to the authorities of the Yerushalmi. Approaching a given rule of the Mishnah, a sage would do one of two things: (1) explain the meaning of the passage, or (2) extend and expand the meaning of the passage. In the former category fall all the items in the first and second approaches, as well as those units of discourse in which either a scriptural proof text is adduced in support of a law or an alleged variant reading of a text is supplied. In the latter category fit all items in the third and fourth approaches, as well as those in which the work is to harmonize laws or principles, on the one side, or to cite and amplify Tosefta's complement to the Mishnah passage, on the other. Within these two categories, which produce, in all, four subdivisions, we may find a place for all units of discourse in which the focus of discussion is a passage of the Mishnah. Of the two sorts, the work of straightforward explanation of the plain meaning of a law of the Mishnah by far predominates. If we may state the outcome very simply: what the framers of the Yerushalmi want to say — whatever else their purpose or aspiration — is what they think the Mishnah means in any given passage. The net effect was to reframe the diverse paragraphs of the Mishnah and recast them within a single limited pattern — metapropositional discourse of a singularly subtle order. For there is no exegetical program revealed in the Yerushalmi's reading of the Mishnah other than that defined, to begin with, by the language and conceptions of one Mishnah passage or another. That makes all the more remarkable the

Yerushalmi's authorship's success in uncovering the deep unities and prevailing harmony of the Mishnah, turning its laws into law: orderly, regular, encompassing, once more the mark of metapropositional discourse. These descriptive remarks take on flesh in the encounter with a concrete passage. For that purpose I turn to the Yerushalmi's treatment of the Mishnah-passage cited in Chapter Four and show how the authorship of the Yerushalmi works its way through the components of that passage. Readers will then see in concrete ways how the general program of systematic and orderly demonstration of a few metapropositions is worked out. The citation of the Mishnah is given in bold-face type, which applies, also, to the Tosefta where introduced. Once more, I give a severely abbreviated selection, sufficient only to establish the main point, concerning a severely limited program of amplification, yielding a many propositions but only a few generalizations or metapropositions.

Yerushalmi Sanhedrin 2.2

A.   And when he gives comfort to others —
B.   the accepted practice is for all the people to pass one after another, and the appointed [perfect of the priests] stands between him and the people.
C.   And when he receives consolation from others,
D.   all the people say to him, "Let us be your atonement."
E.   And he says to them, "May you be blessed by Heaven."
F.   And when they provide him with the funeral meal,
G.   all the people sit on the ground, while he sits on a stool.

I.   A.   [The statement at M. San. 2:2G] implies: A stool is not subject to the law of mourners' overturning the bed.
     B.   [But that is not necessarily so. For] the high priest [to begin with] is subject to that requirement of overturning the bed [and, it follows, no conclusion can be drawn from M.].
          At the outset we want to know whether we may generalize from this case for an unrelated case that may or may not be subject to the same rule. We may not. The premise is that the law is whole and that one part speaks to another.
II. A.   It was taught: They do not bring out the deceased [for burial] at a time near the hour of reciting the Shema, unless they did so an hour earlier or an hour later, so that people may recite the Shema and say the Prayer.
     B.   And have we not learned: When they have buried the dead and returned,

    [If they can begin the Shema and finish it before reaching the row of mourners, they begin it; but if they cannot, they do not begin it[[M. Ber. 3:2]. [Thus they do bring out the deceased for burial at a time quite close to that for reciting the Shema.]

C.   Interpret [the cited pericope of Mishnah] to deal with a case in which the people thought that they had ample time for burying the corpse but turned out not to have ample time for that purpose [prior to the time for reciting the Shema].

D.   It is taught: The person who states the eulogy and all who are involved in the eulogy interrupt [their labor] for the purpose of reciting the Shema, but do not do so for saying the Prayer. M'SH W: Our rabbis interrupted for the purposes of reciting the Shema and saying the Prayer (T. Ber. 2:11).

E.   Now have we not learned, If they can begin and finish ...? [As above, B. Now here we have them interrupt the eulogy!]

F.   The Mishnah refers to the first day [of the death, on which they are exempt from saying the Shema], and the Tosefta pericope to the second [day after death, on which they are liable to say the Shema].

G.   Said R. Samuel bar Abedoma, "This one who entered the synagogue and found the people standing [and saying] the prayer, if he knows that he can complete the Prayer before the messenger of the congregation [who repeats the whole in behalf of the congregation] will begin to answer, 'Amen,' [to the Prayer of the community], he may say the Prayer, and if not, he should not say the Prayer."

H.   To which "Amen" is reference made?

I.   Two Amoras differ in this regard.

J.   One said, "To the Amen which follows, 'The Holy God.'"

K.   And the other said, "to the Amen which follows, 'Who hears prayer' on an ordinary day."

The unstated issue is whether or not the law on the topic at hand is uniform throughout. The answer is that it is. This composition hardly has been worked out in response to our Mishnah-pericope in particular. In what follows, our passage conflicts with a rule given elsewhere — in relationship to the item just now considered — and that accounts for the insertion of the whole, that is, units II and III, in the present location. So the deeper inquiry into the harmonies of the law really defines the stakes, and the location of a composition — whether here, whether at tractate Berakhot — proves adventitious from the viewpoint of those who made up units II-III. But it is central to the program of the authorship of our tractate of the Yerushalmi, and that is critical. What we now learn is that the authorship of the Yerushalmi has drawn upon materials formulated on their own, not in response to the statements of a given passage of the Mishnah but in dialogue with diverse rules that apparently contradict one another. Then that authorship has laid out those materials in accord with the fixed associative principle of sustained discourse. That is to say, what links units I, II-III, and all that follow, in the passage we now survey, is the order of statements of the Mishnah-pericope, M. San. 2:2. The Mishnah-paragraphs establish the connections between completed units of thought.

In intellectual terms we observe diverse processes of thought. Some modes of thought develop propositions on their own; others generate metapropositions, e.g., demonstrations of deep harmonies among diverse laws. Still other exercises in the presentation of the work of intellect join one thing to another solely by reference to a third point of connection, external to the first and the second and unrelated to the purpose for which the first and the second are, on their own, composed — the connection of fixed association, which draws no conclusions and relies upon extrinsic, and not intrinsic, traits of connection and order. The authorship of the Yerushalmi appeals for the composition of the whole to the logic of fixed association, connecting one thing to another through a third, extrinsic points of contact. So it transformed the Mishnah, a document in which connections are made intrinsically, through propositional thought concerning classification and the discovery of prevailing rules, into a sustained and considerable statement that makes sense, in the aggregate, only through appeal to external and extrinsic points of cogency between one thing and something else. But again, and for the last time, I have moved ahead of my tale. Let us revert to our survey of the Yerushalmi's reading of the Mishnah-passage before us, to see how a set-program of implicit propositions tells the authorship what it wishes to know, and say, about the Mishnah-passage at hand, here, harmonization of concrete rules that appear to conflict, demonstration of the inner coherence of the law as a whole. We proceed to yet another passage, once more to show, first, the presence of a uniform program of inquiry, second, the resulting demonstration of propositions deep within the structure of numerous concrete cases.

Yerushalmi Sanhedrin 2:4E-I

E.   "He should not multiply wives to himself" (Deut. 17:17) — only eighteen.

F.   R Judah says, "He may have as many as he wants, so long as they do not entice him [to abandon the Lord (Deut. 7:4)]."

G.   R. Simeon says, "Even if there is only one who entices him [to abandon the Lord] — lo, this one should not marry her."

H.   If so, why is it said, "He should not multiply wives to himself"?

I.   Even though they should be like Abigail [1 Sam. 25:3].

Our first inquiry is into the hermeneutic, stated as a generalization, that underlies the positions of the two disputants. We want to know the principle behind the dispute, and it concerns exegetical rules. The metaproposition, of course, is that wherever there is a dispute between authorities, it concerns a law that applies to more than the case at hand, with the consequence that the law is harmonious and profoundly unified.

I.   A.   Does the dispute [at M. 2:4F, G] bear the implication that R. Judah seeks out the reasoning behind a verse of Scripture, and R. Simeon does not seek out the reasoning behind a verse of Scripture?

B.   But do we not find just the opposite?

C.   For it has been taught on Tannaite authority:

D.   "As to a widow, whether she is poor or rich, people do not exact a pledge from her, for it is said, 'You shall not take the widow's raiment as a pledge' (Deut. 24:17)," the words of R. Judah.

E.   R. Simeon says, "If she is rich, they do exact a pledge from her. If she is poor they do not exact a pledge from her, because one is liable to return it to her, and so may give her a bad name among her neighbors [by constant visitations]."

F.   In that connection we raised the question, What is the sense of that statement?

G.   This is the sense of that statement: Because you take a pledge from her, you are liable to return the object to her, and so you give her a bad name among neighbors [so Simeon].

H.   What follows is that R. Judah does not take account of the reasoning behind a verse of Scripture, and R. Simeon does take account of the reasoning behind a verse of Scripture.

I.   In general R. Judah does not take account of the reasoning behind a verse of Scripture, but the present case is different, for he spells out the reason given in the Scripture itself.

J.   What is the reason that "he shall not multiply wives to himself"? It is because "his heart should not be turned aside."

K.   And R. Simeon? He may reply to you that in general, we do interpret the reason behind a verse of Scripture. In the present case, therefore, the Scripture should have stated, "He should not multiply wives to himself" and then fallen silent. I should then have stated on my own then, "What is the reason that he should not multiply them? So that his heart should not turn away."

L.   Why make "not turning away" explicit therefore?

M.   To indicate, Even if there is only one who entices him to abandon the Lord, lo, this one should not marry her [M. 3:4H].

N.   Then how shall I explain the sense of "He should not multiply"?

O.   Even one like Abigail [M. 2:4I].

II.   A.   As to the number of eighteen [specified at M. 2:4E], what is the source for that number?

B.   It is from the following verse of Scripture: "And unto David were sons born in Hebron, and his first-born son was Amnon, of Ahinoam the Jezreelites, the second, Chileab, of Abigail, the wife of Nabal the Carmelite, the third Absalom, son of Maacah; the fourth, Adonijah, son of Haggith; and the fifth, Shefatiah, son of Abital, and the sixth, Ithream, of Eglah, David's wife. These were born to David in Hebron" (2 Sam. 3:2-5).

C.   And the prophet said to him, "And if that were too little, then would I add to you the like of these and the like of these" (2 Sam. 12:8).

D.   Each "like of these" means six more [since the referent is the original six], so eighteen in all.

E.   Rabina objected, "Might I say that 'Like of these' stands for twelve, and the second such reference means twenty-four [Shachter, p. 113, n. 3: He increased the number in geometrical progression, 6, 12, 24]?"

F.   So it has been taught on Tannaite authority:

G.   "He should not multiply wives to himself" (Deut. 17:17) — more than twenty-four.

H.   In the view of him who interprets the "and," the number is forty-eight.

I.   It has been taught on Tannaite authority along these very lines:

J.   "He should not multiply wives to himself" (Deut. 17:17) — more than forty-eight.

K.   And what is the reason for the view of the Tannaite authority who framed the Mishnah-passage at hand?

L.   Said R. Kahana, "He draws an analogy between the first 'and the like' and the second 'and the like.' Just as the former refers to six, so the latter refers to the six."

M.   But there was Michal [beyond the six wives who are listed]?

N.   Rab said, "Eglah is Michal, and why was she called Eglah? Because she was as beloved of him as a calf [eglah] is of its mother.

O.   "And so it is said, 'If you had not ploughed with my heifer' (Jud. 14:18)."

P.   But did Michal have children? And is it not written, "And Michal, daughter of Saul, had no child to the day of her death" (2 Sam. 6:23)?

Q.   Said R. Hisda, "To the day of her death she had none, but on the day of her death she had one."

R.   Now where, in point of fact, is the number of sons reckoned? It is in Hebron. But the case involving Michal took place in Jerusalem, for it is written, "Michal, daughter of Saul, looked out at the window and saw King David leaping and dancing before the Lord, and she despised him in her heart" (2 Sam. 6:16).

S.   And R. Judah, and some say R. Joseph, said, "Michal took her due punishment, which was childlessness."

T.   Rather, one might propose, prior to that event she had children, but afterward she had none.

U.   [Referring to the issue of the number of eighteen specified in the Mishnah-paragraph], is it not stated, "And David took concubines and wives out of Jerusalem" (2 Sam. 5:13)?

V.   It was to reach the number of eighteen [wives].

W.   What is the difference between wives and concubines?

X.   Said R. Judah said Rab, "Wives are with a marriage contract and a rite of betrothal, concubines are without a marriage contract and without a rite of betrothal."

We conclude with a final demonstration of the principal points on the Yerushalmi's authorship's remarkably cogent way of reading the Mishnah so as to demonstrate, time and again, a few encompassing principles. But we see, also, a sizable exercise of a different sort as well. It is the composition of propositional paragraphs in a sequence dictated not by the requirements of a sustained demonstration of a large-scale case but by the principle of fixed association. That is to say, everything finds its place in the sequence and order dictated not by the logic of propositional argument but by the order of sentences in the Mishnah.

Let me now summarize what we have learned about the methodical-analytical program brought by the authorship of the Yerushalmi (and the Bavli later on) to the Mishnah. The Yerushalmi invariably does to the Mishnah one of these four things: (1) text criticism; (2) exegesis of the meaning of the Mishnah, including glosses and amplifications; (3) addition of scriptural proof texts of the Mishnah's central propositions; and (4) harmonization of one Mishnah passage with another such passage or with a statement of Tosefta.

The first two of these four procedures remain wholly within the narrow frame of the Mishnah passage subject to discussion. The second pair take an essentially independent stance vis-a-vis the Mishnah pericope at hand. The Mishnah is read by the Yerushalmi as a composite of discrete and essentially autonomous rules, a set of atoms, not an integrated molecule, so to speak. In so doing, the most striking formal traits of the Mishnah are obliterated. More important, the Mishnah as a whole and complete statement of a viewpoint no longer exists. Its propositions are reduced to details, pointing toward larger propositions entirely. On occasion, the details may be restated in generalizations encompassing a wide variety of other details across the gaps between one tractate and another. This immensely creative and imaginative approach to the Mishnah vastly expands the range of discourse. But the first, and superficial, consequence is to deny to the Mishnah both its own mode of speech and its distinctive and coherent message. At the same time, the second and deeper result is to homogenize the Mishnah's discrete statements within a pattern of reasoned and orderly inquiry imposed by the intellect of the authorship of the Yerushalmi (and Bavli). And from the viewpoint of the present inquiry, that is the important result.

We began with the intent of exploring metapropositional discourse. That discourse in language brings to expression a range of logic that shows unity in diversity, demonstrates that many things follow a single rule, and demonstrates how a few simple propositions underlie many complex statements of fact. That mode of thought seeks connections at the deepest structure of thought and proposes to explain by reference to a single rule a various and vast universe of fact. We saw how metapropositional logic makes a single fabric out of the threads of propositional logic that fill up the loom comprised by one document after another. Sifra and the two Sifrés stood for that large sector of the canonical writings that, all together, serve to make a few fundamental points, applicable to many cases indeed. The two Talmuds, represented for our purposes by a brief abstract of the Yerushalmi, present us with the same phenomenon: systemic and generalizing thinking about the discrete propositional statements presented by the Mishnah. And yet, we noticed, while the two Sifrés and Sifra (among other writings) proved essentially metapropositional in their over all structure, attaining cogency by doing one thing many times and showing the inner simplicity of the outwardly complex propositions at hand, the Yerushalmi — and by extension, the Bavli — does not follow suit. Quite to the contrary, if we had to characterize the paramount logic of cogent discourse of the Yerushalmi, we should have to identify the prevailing principle of joining one statement to another, that is, of making connection, not with propositional, let alone metapropositional, discourse, but with the connection imposed by fixed association, that alone. For while the several units of completed thought connect fact to fact, sentence to sentence, through the shared proposition generated by what is reasoned and syllogistic argument, those units of thought themselves find connection only in their common reference-point, the Mishnah.

The prevailing logics in some documents work in both the parts and the whole, in one and the same way connecting sentence to sentence, and also paragraph to paragraph. In the Mishnah, Genesis Rabbah, and Leviticus Rabbah, the same logic of propositional discourse that links sentence to sentence also links paragraph to paragraph. That is to say, propositions join one fact or sentence to another and make of the whole a single cogent statement. Still broader propositions join one large-scale cogent statement ("paragraph" in the language of the opening sentence) to another cogent statement. The logic of the whole also defines the logic of the parts. And the same is so of the metapropositional discourse that makes the accomplishment of the authorship of Sifra so remarkable and imparts noteworthy force and sustained argument to the discrete statements of the two Si-

frés as well. In all three documents, the metapropositional program
of the parts imparts its character on large stretches of the whole as
well. We may therefore conclude that some documents hold together,
whole and also in part in one and the same way. They will find connections between their sentences and among the compositions of sentences either by systematically setting forth propositions, argued along
the lines of syllogism, worked out through the analysis accomplished
by classification, comparison and contrast, of genus and species, for
instance, and this they will do throughout. Or authorships will impose
a single subterranean program upon data of unlimited diversity and
show, point by point and overall as well, the unities within diverse
facts — documents that persistently make metapropositional points
and all together find cogency through those recurrent exercises of
deep and methodical analysis.

But the Yerushalmi and the Bavli differ, in their basic logic
structure. For the authorships of these writings compose their completed units of thought principally as propositional, or metapropositional statements. The logic, then, connects one fact to another, one
sentence to another, in such a way as to form a proposition. But the
joining of one completed unit of thought ("paragraph," "propositional statement") to another finds connection not in a still larger exercise of propositional discourse but rather by appeal to the connection imposed through the fixed association accomplished by the
framers of the Mishnah or (for the Bavli, as I shall explain) by Moses,
that is to say, by the author of Scripture. That mixing of two logics, the
propositional for medium-range discourse, the fixed associative for
large-scale composition, differentiates the two Talmuds from all other
canonical writings. Having reached that point, we turn forthwith to
documents that uniformly appeal to the logic of fixed association for
the making of connections (there is, then, no drawing of conclusions), and, once more, we revert to the two Talmuds and their mixture of two logics in the composition of thought, the definition of the
mind of Judaism.

CHAPTER SIX

FIXED-ASSOCIATIVE DISCOURSE

The logic of fixed association connects otherwise unrelated sequential sentences, and also joins into sizable compositions entire paragraphs that in no way coalesce into protracted statements of a cogent character. Among the documents that reached closure prior to the conclusion of the Bavli, few are wholly put together in such a way that the logic of fixed association prevails both in composing sentences into paragraphs and also in establishing the intelligible connection and order of large units of thought, that is, whole paragraphs, whether propositional or otherwise. But we may point to small components of any number of writings in which the logic of fixed association — appeal to some external principle of connection, beyond the range of proposition — prevails. One such instance, among many, comes to us from Sifré to Deuteronomy, and we do well to review its main points before examining documents wholly or mostly put together by appeal to fixed associations extrinsic to proposition or argument.

The fixed-associative mode of discourse in Sifré to Deuteronomy appeals for cogency between and among discrete sentences to a verse of Scripture -indeed, most of the verses of the book of Deuteronomy. Let us rapidly review the criteria for the logic of fixed association. The negative ones are, first, the sentences, two or more, do not all together yield a statement that transcends the sum of the parts. Fact 1, fact 2 will not yield fact 3 (or proposition A). The two facts remain just what they were: unrelated facts. Fixed associative compositions, it follows, do not gain cogency through statements of propositions. The sentences are cogent, but the cogency derives from a source other than shared propositions or participation in an argument yielding a shared proposition. The fixed association derives, it follows from a "text" outside of the composition at hand and known to, taken for granted by, the composition at hand. That "text" may be a list of names; it may be a received document or portion there of. But it is the given, and its cogency is the single prevailing premise that otherwise unrelated facts belong together in some sort of established sequence and order. For fine examples of cogent discourse that rests solely upon fixed associations I refer to this simple instance.

Sifré to Deuteronomy CLXXVIII:III
1. A.   "…the prophet has uttered it presumptuously:"
    B.   One is liable for acting presumptuously, and one is not liable for acting in error.

2. A.   "…do not stand in dread of him:"
    B.   Do not hesitate to hold him guilty as charged.

Each numbered unit forms a single declarative sentence. No. 1 makes a distinction important only in legal theory, and No. 2 simply exhorts people to enforce the law. Nothing joins No. 1 to No. 2 except that both rest upon clauses of the same verse. The compositor of the passage took for granted that that fixed association validated his joining No. 1 to No. 2.

One application of the logic of fixed association therefore draws upon an extrinsic text. We have already noted a second, comprising a fixed list of names, e.g., The Fathers 1:1-3, cited above. But the bulk of The Fathers, e.g., Chapters Three and Four, does not join its discrete sentences through a clearly fixed, received order of names of authorities; I see little rhyme or reason in the way in which the sayings in those two chapters are joined, since to me it seems haphazard. But that is not a problem for our attention in this context. The upshot is that I cannot represent The Fathers as a document wholly conforming to the principle of cogency supplied by a received repertoire of items standing in a fixed association with one another. One portion of its materials does, another does not, adhere in that way.

Yet a third point of fixed association will join together sentences that are connected not in theme let alone in proposition but solely in the name of the authority who said them. Here are instances in The Fathers:

1:12 Hillel and Shammai received [the Torah] from them. Hillel says: Be disciples of Aaron, loving peace and pursuing grace, loving people and drawing them near to the Torah.

13. He would say [in Aramaic]: A name made great is a name destroyed, and one who does not add, subtracts.
   And who does not learn is liable to death. And the one who uses the crown, passes away.

14. He would say: If I am not for myself, who is for me? And when I am for myself, what am I? And if not now, when?

Nothing joins the several statements assigned to Hillel, no common theme, assuredly no single syllogism to be proven on the basis of facts that are adduced. The Mishnah contains a tiny proportion of materials joined solely by reason of the name(s) of authorities, e.g., tractate Eduyyot, and the Yerushalmi and Bavli have some sizable compositions in which only the name, and not the theme or (all the more so) the proposition, serves to link one sentence to another. To show the difference between appeal to a name alone for cogency and use of a shared theme or even a proposition, let me point to a composition in which three sayings make essentially the same point, which is to listen and shut up:

1:17. Simeon his son says: All my life I grew up among the sages, and I found nothing better for a person [the body] than silence. And not the learning is the thing, but the doing. And whoever talks too much causes sin.

Here is yet a further instance in which the several sentences focus upon a shared theme and make one fundamental point.

2:1. Rabbi says: What is the straight path which a person should choose for himself? Whatever is an ornament to the one who follows it, and an ornament in the view of others. Be meticulous in a small religious duty as in a large one, for you do not know what sort of reward is coming for any of the various religious duties. And reckon with the loss [required] in carrying our a religious duty against the reward for doing it; and the reward for committing a transgression against the loss for doing it. And keep your eye on three things, so you will not come into the clutches of transgression. Know what is above you. An eye which sees, and an ear which hears, and all your actions are written down in a book.

Overall, in my view, beyond The Fathers Chapter One we shall look in vain for evidence that, by making a single point or even discussing a single theme, or even by joining together names of authorities in some sort of fixed order, the framers of the document found cogency between two or more sentences. The generally prevailing logic will assemble diverse, thematically only loosely-connected, sayings, which join together merely because the same authority is supposed to have said them — an extreme, but not uncommon, way of connecting one thing with something else. Here is a final example:

2:2. Rabban Gamaliel, a son of Rabbi Judah the Patriarch says: Fitting is learning in Torah along with a craft, for the labor put into the two of them makes one forget sin. And all learning of Torah which is not joined with labor is destined to be null and causes sin. And all who work with the community -let them work with them [the community] for the sake of Heaven. For the merit of the fathers strengthens them, and the righteousness which they do stands forever. And, as for you, I credit you with a great reward, as if you had done [all the work required by the community].

3.   Be wary of the government, for they get friendly with a person only for their own convenience. They look like friends when it is to their benefit, but they do not stand by a person when he is in need.

4.   He would say: Make His wishes into your own wishes, so that He will make your wishes into His wishes. Put aside your wishes on account of His wishes, so that He will put aside the wishes of other people in favor of your wishes. Hillel says: Do not walk out on the community. And do not have confidence in yourself until the day you die. And do not judge your companion until you are in his place. And do not say anything which cannot be heard, for in the end it will be heard. And do not say: When I have time, I shall study, for you may

never have time.

5. He would say: A coarse person will never fear sin, nor will an am ha-Ares ever be pious, nor will a shy person learn, nor will an ignorant person teach, nor will anyone too occupied in business get wise. In a place where there are no individuals, try to be in individual.

6. Also, he saw a skull floating on the water and said to it [in Aramaic]: Because you drowned others, they drowned you, and in the end those who drowned you will be drowned.

7. He would say: Lots of meat, lots of worms; lots of property, lots of worries; lots of women, lots of witchcraft; lots of slave girls, lots of lust; lots of slave boys, lots of robbery. Lots of Torah, lots of life; lots of discipleship, lots of wisdom; lots of counsel, lots of understanding; lots of righteousness, lots of peace. [If] one has gotten a good name, he has gotten it for himself. [If] he has gotten teachings of Torah, he has gotten himself life eternal.

This is a fine example of a potpourri of sentences, linked into a composition solely because all of them are hung onto the name of one authority. While some of the sentences make quite cogent points, and all of them are surely intelligible as discrete statements, the lot of them form a chaotic compost, except that the authorship of the document assigns them to the rubric defined by the named authority. That instance of the logic of fixed association shows us the radical limitations of the mode of thought that joins A to 3 because both A and 3 refer back to a common point, represented here by the symbol #. That mode of thought is fundamentally alien to the orderly pursuit of logical inquiry familiar in the Western philosophical and scientific tradition, because, carried to its logical conclusion, that logic never requires its practitioner to make connections; these are invariably supplied, imputed, never discovered, never source of stimulus to curiosity.

These concrete instances of diverse realizations of the logic of fixed association in hand, we turn to two documents that, in the aggregate, appeal for cogency of two or more sentences and still larger blocks of material to an external set of associated formulas, whether lists of names, repertoires of facts, such as historical events of holy days within the synagogue calendar, preserved in a fixed list, or received documents, e.g., verses of Scripture, sentences of the Mishnah. The first of these two documents is the Tosefta, which is put together as a whole and in many large blocks of completed discourse solely in relationship to the fixed associations defined by the Mishnah. That is to say, in much, though not all, of the Tosefta, why one sentence or set of sentences comes before or after another, and how one relates to another, becomes evident only when we open the Mishnah. There we find that the Tosefta's sentences or groups of sentences very commonly cite and amplify sentences of the Mishnah, or allude to and so state matters as to comment upon, those available sentences. So the connections between one thing and something else run through a different document altogether, a fine instance of the logic of fixed associations in all its extrinsic and formal architecture: a trellis holding up vines from different roots, a building bearing streamers of many colors. I hasten to qualify that the Tosefta also contains some materials formulated not in relationship to the Mishnah's statements at all, and that rather modest proportion of the whole attains cogency between sentence and sentence through appeal to syllogistic argument in behalf of an explicit proposition, pretty much in the same logic manner as do counterpart compositions in the Mishnah. But these do not predominate, and, more to the point, they do not hold the whole together, in the way in which, in Sifré to Deuteronomy or Leviticus Rabbah, propositional discourse forms the core and center of the document as a whole.

The fundamental structure of the Tosefta expresses the same logic of connection as predominates in the joining of its sentences into sustained and (for those who understand things) cogent statements. The Tosefta's tractates follow those of the Mishnah. This is hardly surprising, since Tosefta is a supplement to the Mishnah. When, however, we examine the ways in which Tosefta's tractates are subdivided, we do not see the slightest effort to group materials as do the framers of the Mishnah, that is, in accord with a confluence of common theme and form, or to redact intermediate divisions in accord with a single fixed number of exempla, e.g., three's or five's. Furthermore, Tosefta's units of thought are not highly patterned and exhibit none of the traits of carefully stylized formulation which we find in the Mishnah — except in those pericopae in which the Mishnah itself is cited and glossed (and they are very many). Accordingly, Tosefta, a document dependent on the Mishnah, in no way exhibits careful traits of structured redaction, formal correspondence between formulary patterns and distinctive themes, for the internal demarcation of an intermediate division, or highly formalized formulation of individual units of thought.

Before proceeding, let me give a sizable extract of the Tosefta, the passage that serves the Mishnah-paragraph we considered in our examination of the discourse of propositional logic, and, again, the discourse of metapropositional methodical analysis as well. Here we see a sustained passage of the Tosefta. The reader should notice two points. First, we shall see where and how the Mishnah, printed in bold-face type, is introduced, and the way in which the Tosefta's statements find cogency not in their propositional intersections with one another, e.g., in an orderly sequence of logically sequential topics of problems (first solve this problem, then ask that secondary, and consequent, question). They find order and proportion mainly in their shared relationship to the Mishnah. Second, we want to know where and how the individual sentences of the Tosefta-chapter establish connections with one another to comprise paragraphs, sustained discourse that make points and demonstrate propositions. Overall, we shall notice that the several sentences stand mostly autonomous of one another.

We start with a sustained propositional discussion, which, in its logical and formal traits, can have found a comfortable place in the Mishnah.

4:1 A.   A high priest who committed homicide —
   B.   [if he did so] deliberately, he is executed; if he did so, inadvertently, he goes into exile to the cities of refuge [Num. 35:9ff].
   C.   [If] he transgressed a positive or negative commandment or indeed any of the commandments, lo, he is treated like an ordinary person in every respect.

But of a sudden, we jump into a different discourse altogether. The subject has changed. D stands on its own, unrelated to C.

D.   He does not perform the rite of removing the shoe [Deut. 25:7-9], and others do not perform the rite of removing the shoe with his wife [vs. M. San. 2:1C].

E.   He does not enter into levirate marriage, and [others] do not enter into levirate marriage with his wife [cf. M. San. 2:1C-E].

Once more the subject changes, and the sentences hold together only when we know that the Mishnah's sequence and order defines those of the Tosefta as well.

F.   [When] he stands in the line [to receive comfort as a mourner], the prefect of the priests is at his right hand, and the head of the father's houses [the priestly courses] at his left hand.

G.   And all the people say to him, "Let us be your atonement."

H.   And he says to them. "May you be blessed by Heaven" [M. San. 2:1N-O].

I.   [And when] he stands in the line to give comfort to others, the prefect of the priests and the [high] priest who has now passed out of his position of grandeur are at his right hand, and the mourner is at his left.

J.   [People may] not watch him while he is getting a haircut, [or while he is nude] or in the bathhouse [M. San. 2:5B].

K.   since it is said, And he who is high priest among his brothers (Lev. 21:10) -that his brethren should treat him with grandeur.

L.   But if he wanted to permit others to wash with him, the right is his.

What follows supplements the foregoing. Were the printer not to have marked at break at 4:2A, we should have noticed that there is an abrupt shift in topic from 4:1/O to 4:1P — for which we can account, once more, only by turning back to the Mishnah.

M.   R. Judah says, "If] he wanted to disgrace himself, they do not pay attention to him,

N.   "as it is said, And you will keep him holy (Lev. 21:8) -even against his will."

O.   They said to R. Judah, "To be sure [Scripture] says, From the Temple he shall not go forth (Lev. 21:12), [but this is referring] only to the time of the Temple service" [M. San. 2:1I-J].

P.   He goes out to provide a funeral meal for others, and others come to provide a funeral meal for him.

4.2   A.   An Israelite king does not stand in line to receive comfort [in the time of bereavement],

B.   nor does he stand in line to give comfort to others.

C.   And he does not go to provide a funeral meal for others.

D.   But others come to him to give a funeral meal [M. San. 2:3F],

E.   as it is said, And the people went to provide a funeral meal for David (II Sam. 3:35).

F.   And if he transgressed a positive or a negative commandment or indeed any of the commandments, lo, he is treated like an ordinary person in every respect.

G.   He does not perform the rite of removing the shoe, and others do not perform the rite of removing the shoe with his wife.;

H.   he does not enter into levirate marriage, nor [do his brothers] enter into levirate marriage with his wife [M. San. 2:2C-D].

I.   R. Judah says, "If he wanted to perform the rite of removing the shoe [M. San. 2:9, he has the right to do so."

J.   They said to him, "You turn out to do damage to the glory owing to a king."

K.   And [others] do not marry his widow [M. San. 2:3G], as it is said, So they were shut up to the day of their death, living in widowhood (II Sam. 20:3).

L.   And he has the right to choose wives for himself from any source he wants, whether daughters of priests, Levites, or Israelites.

M.   And they do not ride on his horse, sit on his throne, handle his crown or scepter or any of his regalia [M. San. 2:5].

N.   [When] he dies, all of them are burned along with him, as it is said, You shall die in peace and with the burnings of your fathers, the former kings (Jer. 34:5).

What follows is a cogent statement, entirely connected within the terms of its own proposition: a set of rules on the conduct of the king. These materials can have found a home in the Mishnah-chapter we reviewed above. Yet, we realize, with the Mishnah in hand, we understand the full context and can grasp the deep premises on which these statements are made.

4.3   A.   Just as they make a burning for kings [who die], so they make a burning for patriarchs [who die].

      B.   But they do not do so for ordinary people.

      C.   What do they burn on their account?

      D.   Their bed and other regalia.

4.4   A.   Everybody stands, while he sits.

      B.   And sitting was [permitted] in the Temple courtyard only for kings of the house of David.

C.   All the people keep silent, when he is talking.

D.   He would call them, "My brothers" and "My people," as it is said, Hear you, my brothers and my people (I Chron. 28:2).

E.   And they call him, "Our Lord and our master,"

F.   as it is said, But our Lord David, the King, has made Solomon king (I Kings 1:43).

4.5 A.   "He should not multiply wives for himself (Deut. 17:17) -like Jezebel. But [if the wives are like] Abigail, it is permitted," the words of R. Judah [vs. M. San. 2:4H-I].

B.   He should not multiply horses for himself (Deut. 17:16) -if the horses are left idle, even one [he may not keep],

C.   as it is said, Lest he multiply horses.

D.   R. Judah says, "Lo, it says, And Solomon had forty thousand stalls of horses (I Kings 4:26) -yet he did well,

E.   "for it is written, And Judah and Israel were as many as the sand that is on the seashore for multitude(I Kings 4:20).

F.   "And since it is written, Twelve thousand horsemen (I Kings 4:26), one has to conclude that the rest of the horses were left idle."

G.   But an ordinary person is permitted [to do] all of these things.

H.   R. Yosé says, "Everything that is spelled out in the pericope of the king (Deut. 17:14) is [an ordinary person] permitted to do."

I.   R. Judah says, "That pericope is written only to make the people revere him [cf. M. San 2:5C],

J.   "for it is written, You will surely set a king over you (Deut. 17:14)."

From this point forward, the framers of the passage have gone their own way. I present the remainder of the thematically-pertinent chapter of the Tosefta, because it allows us to see the large-scale principle of organization and composition of the document as a whole. Specifically, the framers of the Tosefta tended to order materials in accord with their relationship to the Mishnah. They present, first in sequence, those materials that cite and gloss sentences of the Mishnah. Then they insert materials that do not cite the Mishnah verbatim, but that do amplify or otherwise clarify rules that the Mishnah gives. Finally, they tack on compositions that are essentially autonomous of the Mishnah. These go on to topics of their own choosing and register propositions that the framers of the Mishnah do not even consider in the present context. What that sequence of three types of material, ordered in accord with their relationship to the Mishnah, indicates, is that the principle of composing the Tosefta as a whole derives from the fundamental relationships established by the document of fixed association, the Mishnah. So when we point to a document that, in its fundamental construction and structure, rests upon the logic of fixed association, that is no trivial matter. I present the remainder to show how, once discussion of the Mishnah, cited verbatim, then of themes shared with the Mishnah, has concluded, the framers go on their own way. It is the order of types of material, classified by their relationship to the Mishnah, that dictates the arrangement of the whole — just as is the case, overall, in the two Talmuds. But here too, in some modest measure, we find that the connections between and among sentences, or facts, of which sizable units of discourse are made up, are established through propositional discourse, in which connections are made to yield conclusions, even while the whole joins together on another logical basis entirely. What follows can have found a comfortable position in the Mishnah as much as in any other propositional composition. I give a sizable sample, to underline the diverse character of Tosefta's units of discourse, and to point to yet another way in which the authorship of the Tosefta has turned to the Mishnah for the fundamental structure and order of its composition.

K. And so did R. Judah say, "Three commandments were imposed upon the Israelites when they came into the land.

L. "They were commanded to appoint a king, to build the chosen house, and to cut off the descendants of Amalek.

M. "If so, why were they punished in the days of Samuel [for wanting a king]? Because they acted too soon."

N. R. Nehorai says, "This pericope was written only because of [future] complaints [with the king].

O. "For it is said, And you will say, I will set a king over me (Deut. 17:14)."

P. R. Eleazar b. R. Yosé says, "The elders asked in the proper way, as it is said, "Give us a king to judge us (I Sam. 8:6).

Q. "But the ordinary folk went and spoiled matters, as it is said, That we also may be like all the nations, and our king will judge us and go before us to fight our battles (I Sam. 8:20)."

4.6 A. "Those put to death by the court — their property goes to their heirs.

B. "But those put to death by the king -their property goes to the king," [the words of R. Judah].

C.   And sages say, "Those put to death by their king -their property goes to their heirs."

D.   Said R. Judah to them, "It says, Behold, he [Ahab] is in the vineyard of Naboth, where he has gone down to take possession (I Kings 21:18)."

E.   They said to him, "It was because he was the son of his father's brother [and] it was appropriate [to come] to him as in inheritance."

F.   They said to him, "And did [Naboth] have no children?"

G.   They said to him, "And did he not kill both him and his children,

H.   "as it is said, Surely I have seen yesterday the blood of Naboth and the blood of his sons, says the Lord; and I will requite you in this plot, says the Lord (Ii Kings 9:26)?"

4.7 A.   And he writes for himself a scroll of the Torah (Deut. 17:17) —

B.   for his own use, that he not have to make use of the one of his fathers, but rather of his own,

C.   as it is said, And he will write for himself —

D.   that the very writing of the scroll should be for him [in particular].

E.   And an ordinary person has no right to read in it,

F.   as it is said, And he will read in it —

G.   he, and no one else.

H.   And they examine [his scroll] in the court of the priests, in the court of the Levites, and in the court of the Israelites who are of suitable genealogical character to marry into the priesthood.

I.   [When] he goes to war, it is with him, when he comes back, it is with him [cf. M. San. 2:4M]; when he goes to court it is with him; when he goes to the urinal, it waits for him [outside] at the door,

J.   and so does David say, I have set God always before me [and he is on my right hand] (Ps. 16:8).

K.   R. Judah says, "A scroll of the Torah as at his right hand, and Tefillin are on his arm."

L.   R. Yosé said, "Ezra was worthy for the Torah to have been given by him, had not Moses come before him.

M.   "Concerning Moses going up is stated, and concerning Ezra going up is stated.

N.   "Concerning Moses going up is stated, as it is said, And Moses went up to God (Ex. 19:3).

O.   "And concerning Ezra going up is stated, as it is written, And he, Ezra, when up from Babylonia (Ezra 7:6).

P.   "Just as, in the case of going up mentioned in connection with Moses, he taught Torah to Israel, as it is stated, And the Lord commanded me at that time to teach you statutes and judgments (Deut. 4:14),

Q.   "so, in the case of going up mentioned in connection with Ezra, he taught

Torah to Israel, as it is said, For Ezra had prepared his heart to expound the law of the Lord and to do it and to teach in Israel statutes and judgments (Ezra 7:0)."

R. Also through him were given [both] a form of writing and language, as it is said, And the writing of the letter was written in the Aramaic character and interpreted in the Aramaic tongue (Ezra 4:7).

S. Just as its interpretation was in Aramaic, so its writing was in Aramaic.

T. And it says, "But they could not read the writing, nor make known to the king the interpretation thereof (Dan. 5:8) —

U. this teaches that on that very day it was given.

V. And it ways, And he shall write a copy of this law (Deut. 17:18) -A Torah which is destined to be changed.

W. And why was [the language] called Assyrian? Because it came up with them from Assyria.

X. Rabbi says, "In Assyrian writing was the Torah given to Israel, and when they sinned, it was changed to Ro'as.

Y. "But when they attained merit in the time of Ezra, Assyrian returned to them, as it is said, Turn you to the stronghold, you prisoners of hope, even today do I declare that I will bring back -the change unto you (Zech. 9:12).

4.8 A. R. Simeon b. Eleazar says in the name of R. Eleazar b. Parta who said it in the name of R. Eleazar of Modiin, "In the present kind of writing the Torah was given to Israel, as it says, The hooks (vavs) of the pillars (Ex. 27:10) -vavs that are written like pillars.

B. "And it says, And unto the Jews according to their writing and language (Est. 8:9) -Just as their language has not changed, so their writing has not changed.

C. "And why is it called Assyrian (ashur)? Because they are upright (me'usharim) in their manner of shaping letters."

D. If so, why is it said, And he shall write for himself a copy of this law (Deut. 17:17)?

E. This teaches that he writes for himself two Torahs, one which comes in with him and goes out with him, and one which he leaves home.

F. This one which goes out and comes in with him should not go in with him to the bathhouse or the urinal, as it is said, And it shall be with him and he shall read in it all the days of his life -that is to say, in a place in which it is appropriate for reading [M. San. 2:4M-N].

G. And does this not produce an argument a fortiori:

H. Now if of an Israelite king, who is busy only with his public duties, it is said, And it shall be with him and he shall read therein all the days of his life,

I. the rest of the people, all the more so [should they have and read Torah-scrolls].

4.9 A. Similarly you say: And Joshua the son of Nun was full of the spirit of wisdom, for Moses had laid his hand upon him (Deut. 34:9)

B. And so it says, And his minister, Joshua, the son of Nun, a young man, stirred not from the midst of the tent (Ex. 33:11).

C. And so it says [even to him], This book of the Torah shall not depart out of your mouth (Josh. 1:8) —

D. the rest of the people, all the more so [should they have and read Torah-scrolls].

4.10 A. They do not appoint a king outside of the Land.

B. They appoint a king only if he was married into the priesthood.

C. And they anoint kings only over a spring.

D. as it is said, And he said to them, Take with you the servants of your lord and mount Solomon, my son, upon my own mule, and bring him down to Gihon (I Kings 1:33).

4.11 A. They anoint kings only on account of civil strife.

B. Why did they anoint Solomon? Because of the strife of Adonijah.

C. And Jehu? Because of Joram.

D. And Joash? Because of Athaliah.

E. And Jehoahaz? Because of Jehoiakim his brother, who was two years older than he.

F. A king requires anointing, [but] a son of a king does not require anointing.

G. A high priest, son of a high priest, even up to the tenth generation, [nonetheless] requires anointing.

H. And they anoint kings only from a horn.

I. Saul and Jehu were anointed from a flask, because their rule was destined to be broken.

J. David and Solomon were anointed from a horn, because their dominion is an eternal dominion.

Let me now generalize on the interplay of the Mishnah and the Tosefta . This will allow us to see the full dimensions of the dependence of the Tosefta upon the Mishnah for order and structure. The Mishnah's traits emerge most clearly in the contrast established by comparing the Mishnah to its supplementary document. The mode of grouping cognitive units in Tosefta is in accord with one of three fixed relationships to the Mishnah. Pericopae which cite the Mishnah verbatim will stand together. There commonly will follow units which do not cite the Mishnah but which clearly complement the principal document, augmenting its materials in some obvious ways. And, at the end will be grouped together still other groups which supplement the Mishnah but which in no clear way depend upon the Mishnah for full and exhaustive exegesis. Accordingly, Tosefta's arrangement of its materials clearly relates to the Mishnah; and the contrast in the ways in which the Mishnah's own groups of cognitive units are set forth could not be more blatant. It follows that the Tosefta's fundamental logic of connection, small bits to other small bits, groups of small bits to other such groups, is one and the same, namely, the logic of fixed association. Without the Mishnah, the Tosefta falls to pieces, enjoying no logic of cogent discourse at all.

Now as to our inquiry into the Talmuds as documents composed, in the making of their medium- and large-scale logical connections, in accord with two distinct principles. These are, we recall, first, the one of propositional connection within completed units of thought, a connection discovered through the pursuit of reasoned speculative inquiry, and second, the other of the fixed associative connection between and among those same completed units of thought, producing large-scale compositions. Sizable numbers of the completed units of thought of the Yerushalmi, all the more so of the Bavli, find inner cogency through the development of a proposition concerning a given theme. Overall, these units of completed thought are linked to one another through the connections supplied extrinsically by the Mishnah, for the Yerushalmi, and, as I shall explain, by both the Mishnah and Scripture, for the Bavli.

The framers of the Bavli had in hand a tripartite corpus of inherited materials awaiting composition into a final, closed document. First, they took up materials, in various states and stages of completion, pertinent to the Mishnah or to the principles of laws that the Mishnah had originally brought to articulation. Second, they had in hand received materials, again in various conditions, pertinent to the Scripture, both as the Scripture related to the Mishnah and also as the Scripture laid forth its own narratives. Finally, they had in hand materials focused on sages. These were framed around twin biographical principles, either as strings of stories about great sages of the past or as collections of sayings and comments drawn together solely because the same name stands behind the sayings. The decision the framers of the Bavli reached was to adopt the two redactional principles inherited from the antecedent century or so and to reject the one already rejected by their predecessors, even while honoring it. And that points to the way in which the logic of fixed association governed their work.

Before proceeding, let me give an example of the way in which I conceive the Bavli's framers to have made usc of the logic of fixed association in that dual way that involved appeal for cogency to both the Mishnah and Scripture. Once more I turn to a familiar item, namely, Mishnah-tractate Sanhedrin Chapter Two, now as the Bavli's authorship presents matter. Since our interest is in identifying passages in which both the Mishnah and Scripture serve to hold together discrete compositions, ordinarily of a propositional character, I give only highlights. These will then illustrate the workings of the logic of fixed association in the Bavli. The numbers in square brackets refer to the Bavli's pagination. Mishnah- and Tosefta-citations are given in bold face type.

Bavli-tractate Sanhedrin to Mishnah-tractate Sanhedrin 2:3

A. [If] [the king] suffers a death in his family, he does not leave the gate of his palace.
B. R. Judah says, "If he wants to go out after the bier, he goes out,
C. "for thus we find in the case of David, that he went out after the bier of Abner,
D. "since it is said, 'And King David followed the bier' (2 Sam. 3:31)."
E. They said to him, "This action was only to appease the people."
F. And when they provide him with the funeral meal, all the people sit on the ground, while he sits on a couch.

I.

A. Our rabbis have taught on Tannaite authority:
B. In a place in which women are accustomed to go forth after the bier, they go forth in that way. If they are accustomed to go forth before the bier, they go forth in that manner.
C. R. Judah says, "Women always go forth in front of the bier.
D. "For so we find in the case of David that he went forth after the bier of Abner.
E. "For it is said, 'And King David followed the bier' (2 Sam. 3:31)."

F.   They said to him, "That was only to appease the people [M. 2:3D-E].

G.   "They were appeased, for David would go forth among the men and come in among the women, go forth among the women and come in among the men,

H.   "as it is said, 'So all the people and all Israel understood that it was not of the king to slay Abner' (2 Sam. 3:37)."

The Bavli's authorship now inserts a sizable exposition on David's relationship with Abner, and this goes its own way, without regard to the amplification of M. Sanhedrin 2:3D-E, cited just now. The following not-very-cogent unit of discourse makes no single point but holds together because of the systematic amplification of the cited verses. No. II stands by itself and sets the stage for what is to follow.

II.

A.   Raba expounded, "What is the meaning of that which is written, 'And all the people came to cause David to eat bread' (2 Sam. 3:35)?

B.   "It was written, 'to pierce David' [with a K], but we read, 'to cause him to eat bread' [with a B].

C.   "To begin with they came to pierce him but in the end to cause him to eat bread."

Now we proceed with the theme of David and Abner.

III.

A.   Said R. Judah said Rab, "On what account was Abner punished? Because he could have prevented Saul but did not prevent him [from killing the priest of Nob, 1 Sam. 22:18]."

B.   R. Isaac said, "He did try to prevent him, but he got no response."

C.   And both of them interpret the same verse of Scripture: "And the king lamented for Abner and said, Should Abner die as a churl dies, your hands were not bound or your feet put into fetters" (2 Sam. 2:33).

D.   He who maintains that he did not try to stop Saul interprets the verse in this way: "Your hands were not bound nor were your feet put into fetters" -so why did you not try to stop him? "As a man falls before the children of iniquity so did you fall" (2 Sam. 3:33).

E.   He who maintains that he did try to stop Saul but got no response interprets the verse as an expression of amazement: "Should he have died as a churl dies? Your hands were not bound and your feet were not put into fetters."

F.   Since he did protest, why "As a man falls before the children of iniquity, so did you fall"?

G. In the view of him who has said that he did protest, why was he punished?

H. Said R. Nahman bar Isaac, "Because he held up the coming of the house of David by two and a half years."

The framer reverts to the Mishnah-passage and proceeds. What we have now is the familiar program of Mishnah-exegesis: amplification of words and phrases in the instance of No. IV, of which I present only a few stichs.

IV.

A. And when they provide him with the funeral meal, [all the people sit on the ground, while he sits on a couch] [M. 2:3F]:

B. What is the couch?

C. Said Ulla, "It is a small couch [Shachter, p. 106, n. 3: not used for rest but placed in the home merely as an omen of good fortune]."

D. Said rabbis to Ulla, "Now is there something on which, up to that time, he had never sat, and now we seat him on that object?"

E. Raba objected to this argument, "What sort of problem is this? Perhaps it may be compared to the matter of eating and drinking, for up to this point we gave him nothing to eat or drink, while now we bring him food and drink...."

The on-going discussion of the matter provides a secondary development of the rules pertaining to the couch under discussion and need not detain us. Yet another example of a sizable composition appealing for cogency to Scripture is tacked on to M. 2:4A-D. Here is another composition that holds together solely because of reference to verses of Scripture. Specifically, 2 Sam. 13 forms the center, and the various sentences then are joined to that center, but not to one another:

III.

A. Said R. Judah said Rab, "David had four hundred sons, all of them born of beautiful captive women. All grew long locks plaited down the back. All of them seated in golden chariots.

B. "And they went forth at the head of troops, and they were the powerful figures in the house of David."

C. And R. Judah said Rab said, "Tamar was the daughter of a beautiful captive woman.

D. "For it is said, 'Now, therefore, I pray you, speak to the king, for he will not withhold me from you' (2 Sam. 13:13).

E. "Now if you hold that she was the daughter of a valid marriage, would the king ever have permitted [Amnon] to marry his sister?

F. "But, it follows, she was the daughter of a beautiful captive woman."

G. "And Amnon had a friend, whose name was Jonadab, son of Shimeah, David's brother, and Jonadab was a very subtle man" (2 Sam. 13:3): Said R. Judah said Rab, "He was subtle about doing evil."

H. "And he said to him, Why, son of the king, are you thus becoming leaner... And Jonadab said to him, Lay down on your bed and pretend to be sick... and she will prepare the food in my sight... and she took the pan and poured [the cakes] out before him" (2 Sam. 13:4ff.): Said R. Judah said Rab, "They were some sort of pancakes."

I. "Then Amnon hated her with a very great hatred" (2 Sam. 13:15): What was the reason?

J. Said R. Isaac, "One of his hairs got caught [around his penis and cut it off] making him one whose penis had been cut off."

K. But was she the one who had tied the hair around his penis? What had she done?

L. Rather, I should say, she had tied a hair around his penis and made him into one whose penis had been cut off.

M. Is this true? And did not Raba explain, "What is the sense of the verse, 'And your renown went forth among the nations for your beauty' (Ez. 16:14)? It is that Israelite women do not have armpit or pubic hair."

N. Tamar was different, because she was the daughter of a beautiful captive woman.

O. "And Tamar put ashes on her head and tore her garment of many colors" (2 Sam. 13:19):

P. It was taught on Tannaite authority in the name of R. Joshua b. Qorhah, "Tamar established a high wall at that time [protecting chastity]. People said, 'If such could happen to princesses, all the more so can it happen to ordinary women.' If such could happen to virtuous women, all the more so can it happen to wanton ones!"

Q. Said R. Judah said Rab, "At that time they made a decree [21B] against a man's being alone with any woman [married or] unmarried."

R. But the rule against a man's being along with [a married woman] derives from the authority of the Torah [and not from the authority of rabbis later on].

S. For R. Yohanan said in the name of R. Simeon b. Yehosedeq, "Whence in the Torah do we find an indication against a man's being alone [with a married woman]? As it is said, 'If your brother, of your mother, entice you' (Deut. 13:7).

T. "And is it the fact that the son of one's mother can entice, but the son of the father cannot entice? Rather, it is to tell you that a son may be alone with his mother, and no one else may be alone with any of the consanguineous female relations listed in the Torah."

U.   Rather, they made a decree against a man's being alone with an unmarried woman.

V.   "And Adonijah, son of Haggith, exalts himself, saying, I will be king" (1 Kgs. 1:5):

W.   Said R. Judah said Rab, "This teaches that he tried to fit [the crown on his head], but it would not fit."

X.   "And he prepares chariots and horses and fifty men to run before him" (1 Kgs. 1:5):

Y.   So what was new [about princes' having retinues]?

Z.   Said R. Judah said Rab, "All of them had had their spleen removed [believed to make them faster runners] and the flesh of the soles of their feet cut off [Shachter, p. 115, n. 12: so that they might be fleet of foot and impervious to briars and thorns]."

My final example of how Scripture serves to connect one sentence to another shows us, from the citation of the Mishnah onward, a systematic interest not in the Mishnah but in Scripture and its exposition.

2:5

A.   **[Others may] not ride on his horse, sit on his throne, handle his scepter.**

B.   **And [others may] not watch him while he is getting a haircut, or while he is nude, or in the bath-house,**

C.   **since it is said, "You shall surely set him as king over you" (Deut. 17:15) — that reverence for him will be upon you.**

I.

A.   Said R. Jacob said R. Yohanan, "Abishai would have been permitted to be married to Solomon, but was forbidden to be married to Adonijah.

B.   "She would have been permitted to Solomon, because he was king, and the king is permitted to make use of the scepter of [a former] king.

C.   "But she was forbidden to Adonijah, for he was an ordinary person."

II.

A.   And what is the story of Abishai?

B.   It is written, "King David was old, stricken in years... His servants said to him, Let there be sought..." And it is written, "They sought for him a pretty girl..." and it is written, "And the girl was very fair, and she became a companion to the king and ministered to him" (1 Kgs. 1:1-5).

C.   She said to him, "Let's get married."

D.   He said to her, "You are forbidden to me."

E.   She said to him, "When the thief fears for his life, he seizes virtue."

F.   He said to them, "Call Bath Sheba to me."

G.   And it is written, "And Bath Sheba went into the king to the chamber" (1 Kgs. 1:15).

H.   Said R. Judah said Rab, "At that time [having had sexual relations with David] Bath Sheba wiped herself with thirteen cloths [to show that he was hardly impotent, contrary to Abishag's accusation]."

I.   Said R. Shemen bar Abba, "Come and take note of how difficult is an act of divorce.

J.   "For lo, they permitted King David to be alone [with the woman], but they did not permit him to divorce [one of his other wives]."...

The exposition of the Mishnah hardly requires insertion of these materials, the cogency of which derives rather from Scripture. Now let me return to the argument overall and state matters in general terms. A further repertoire of examples of the operation of the logic of fixed association, in the Bavli's case defined by both the Mishnah and Scripture, its themes or its sequential verses, is not required to make the simple point at hand.

The authorships of the tractates of the Bavli in general first of all organized the Bavli around the Mishnah, just as did the framers of the Yerushalmi. But, second, they adapted and included vast tracts of antecedent materials organized as scriptural commentary. These they inserted whole and complete, not at all in response to the Mishnah's program. And, finally, while making provision for compositions built upon biographical principles, preserving both strings of sayings from a given master (and often a given tradent of a given master) as well as tales about authorities of the preceding half millennium, they did nothing new. That is to say, they never created redactional compositions, of a sizable order, that focused upon given authorities, even though sufficient materials lay at hand to allow doing so. In the three decisions, two of what to do and one of what not to do, the final compositors of the Bavli indicated what they proposed to accomplish. It was to give final form and fixed expression, through their categories of the organization of all knowledge, to the Torah as it had been

known, sifted, searched, approved, and handed down, even from the
remote past to their own day. Accordingly, the Bavli's ultimate framers made the decision to present large-scale discussions along lines
of order and sequence dictated not by topics and propositional arguments concerning them — as did Aphrahat, for instance, in his demonstrations. Rather they selected the two components of the one
whole Torah, oral and written, of Moses, our rabbi, at Sinai, and
these they set forth as the connections that held together and ordered
all discourse. That is how they organized what they knew, on the one
side, and made their choices in laying out the main lines of the structure of knowledge, on the other.

The logic of fixed association permitted the Bavli's authorships to appeal to two distinct repertoires of sequential items, the
Mishnah, Scripture. That is why the Bavli as a whole lays itself out as a
commentary to the Mishnah. So the framers wished us to think that
whatever they wanted to tell us would take the form of Mishnah commentary. But a second glance indicates that the document is made up
of enormous composites, themselves closed prior to inclusion in the
Bavli. Some of these composites — around 35% to 40% of Bavli's, if
my sample in Judaism. The Classic Statement. The Evidence of the
Bavli is indicative — were selected and arranged along lines dictated
by a logic other than that deriving from the requirements of Mishnah
commentary. In these the logic of redaction — what (self-evidently)
comes first, what (obviously) goes below -emerges from a different
sort of exegetical task from Mishnah commentary. As I said, people
focused upon passages of Scripture in making up their compositions
of exegesis. And again, as already suggested, sorting out the large-
scale compositions of which the document at hand is made up produces yet a third type of composite, this one drawn together around a
given name and made up of sayings, often on diverse subjects, attributed to that name, or of stories told about that name.

Prior to the work of ultimate composition, closure, and redaction, sizable compositions — we might call them "chapters," that
is, completed statements or units of discourse — took shape in a
number of different ways. We know that because of our survey of the

received canonical documents, generally held by scholarship today to have reached closure prior to the conclusion of the Bavli. There we saw compositions drawn together through diverse propositions, and also those made cogent by appeal to fixed association, whether with verses of Scripture or (as in the Tosefta and Yerushalmi) sentences of the Mishnah. Not only so, but sequences of stories about sages' lives certainly were formed. Fixed association therefore made available non-propositional but (in context) cogent compositions around Scripture, the Mishnah, and the sage, or, to state matters theologically, the written Torah, the oral Torah, and the living Torah. The framers of the Bavli drew together the results of these three types of work, which people prior to their own labors already had created in abundance as both completed documents and also sizable components, statements awaiting agglutination or conglomeration in finished documents.. Using the two I specified as definitive structures of logical connection, and therefore, consequently, also of literary redaction, the framers made of them all one document, the Bavli, or, in the later tradition of Judaism, the Talmud.

Whatever the place and role of the diverse types of compositions circulating before and in the time of the Bavli — compilations of scriptural exegeses, the Yerushalmi, not to mention the exegeses of Pentateuchal laws in Sifra and the Sifrés, the Tosefta, Pirqé Abot and Abot de R. Natan, and on and on — the Bavli superseded them all. It therefore defined the mind of Judaism. Among the two ultimate classifications of logic — propositional and fixed associative — the Bavli appealed for ultimate composition, cogency of all learning, to the latter. It made room for propositional discourse at that middle range of knowledge that made of the parts autonomous statements of one thing or another. But its authorship put all knowledge together not into a series of treatises on topics and propositions, such as Aphrahat provided (and he merely exemplifies a vast world of philosophical thought), but into a series of medium-length discourses that gain cogency imposed only from without. An intellectual world defined in this way found ample stimulus for speculation, but not for that kind of speculation that, to begin with, addressed the issue of connection between one thing and something else. For the Mishnah or Scripture, or even the lives and teachings of holy men, imparted to two or more discrete facts that connection that led to the drawing of conclusions and the framing of theses for inquiry, at least so far as the Bavli's treatises' authorships exemplified the logic defining the mind of Judaism. And, as I shall now argue, it is where connection is discovered, not imputed, that philosophy, including the subdivision of natural philosophy we now know as science, flourishes. In the mind of Judaism, speculation and imagination, among many modes of original and creative thought, would flourish from the Bavli to the present age. But, except for a tiny minority, philosophy, therefore also science, would not. In consequence, only those Jews who abandoned the sciences of Judaism became scientists in the Western sense of the word, while the Jews whose intellects were formed within the canonical literature of Judaism, and, in particular, the Bavli and the intellectual tradition, continuous and on-going from the seventh century to the present day, rarely asked questions as philosophers and scientists ask them, and so produced no science. Let me now make these assertions stick.

CHAPTER SEVEN

WHY NO SCIENCE
IN THE MIND OF JUDAISM?

Thinking in one way and not in another involves the making of connections and the drawing of conclusions in this way, not in that, with the consequence that philosophy, encompassing natural philosophy or science, as we now call it, will or will not emerge. If I make connections in one way, I shall also, by the way, think philosophically and produce science, in both mode of thought and (given the world in which we live, inevitably also) subject-matter, encompassing natural science, and if I make connections in another way, I shall produce other kinds of thought and — in the nature of things — also deal with other subjects entirely. The way in which connections are made between one thing and something also will also affect the things I choose to connect — and then explain. The specific modes of thought that generate philosophical, including scientific, thought in the present context are not difficult to define. Science as a mode of thought bears two distinct, though related meanings: mode of thought, subject matter. It is a way of thinking about the phenomena of nature. Science involves orderly and systematic description and explanation of natural phenomena, which, in my terms, I should call the making of connections between one thing and another and the drawing of conclusions based on the making of connections. And the critical component of science is the making of connections in one way rather than in some other: this relates to that, but this does not relate to the other thing. These connections — and also rejection of connections — are discovered or intuited, then tested empirically. Connection is not supplied, not received, not dictated by convention.

It is science as a mode of thought, encompassing an interest in natural phenomena, that I claim not to find in mind exhibited by the formative stages of the canon of the Judaism of the dual Torah. To state the simple fact: when Jews did science, they disregarded the study of the Torah as the Judaism of the dual Torah expounded it and took up another mode of learning and a different text. Torah-study was not conceived to encompass scientific learning, either as mode of thought (in terms I shall define in a moment) or as a subject-matter. On a broader scale, philosophy, of which natural science formed a part, involved different ways of thinking about different things from the modes of thought concerning God's revealed Torah that the Judaism of the dual Torah, its masters and institutions, studied. And further to state my thesis: the ways of making connections and drawing conclusions, specifically the mixed logics of the dual Torah in its ultimate canonical statement, produced a different sort of learning from the philosophical, the scientific. So while in medieval times learned masters of the Torah also undertook philosophical, including scientific, inquiry, they thought in a different way about different things from the mode of thought and the subject-matter of Torah-study. The indicative traits of mind defined by the canonical writings of the Judaism of the dual Torah explain why the philosophical, including the scientific, mode of thought did not flourish within Jewry so long as that Judaism predominated in the past, and that does not flourish today where that Judaism remains normative.

The Bavli in particular is what defined the mind of Judaism, and to understand how that fact determined the future course of intellect in the community of Judaism, we have to understand the power, but also the pathos, of the intellect defined by the Bavli's authorship. It was, on the one side, profoundly philosophical and highly propositional. Its thinkers aggressively advanced a systematic skepticism, a purifying testing of results. Within its pages are evidences of an interest in empirical testing, and testing allegations against established facts is routine. The Bavli's mind is not meant to produce subservience to authority but active and engaged intellect of a highly critical order. But it was, on the other side, a mode of philosophical thinking that generated thought of one sort and not of another, and disciplined philosophical argument, beginning, middle, and end, was not the principal trait of the Bavli's mode of thought. For reasons absolutely critical to the Bavli's intellectual dynamic, dialectic — the moving argument — and not systematic and orderly argument marked the Bavli's choice of mode of argument and inquiry, and the one fundamental requirement of dialectic is the implicit connection between this and that. Otherwise dialectic degenerates into free association, while yet rational, and, beyond the border of shared discourse, a mere babbling. To explain what I mean will require an account of the intellectual power of the Bavli, why it had the astonishing impact upon the shaping of the intellectual life of the community of Judaism that it has had, and yet retains, since its closure fifteen hundred years ago. Only when we grasp the reasons for the Bavli's strength shall we understand the basis, also, for its limitations. Let me spell out what I conceive to be the indicative traits of mind that yielded thought of one sort and not of another for the Bavli's statement of the Judaism of the dual Torah.

Let me first dismiss as false the explanation for the absence of science, including philosophy, from Judaism that the Bavli's basic mode of thought was unsystematic because it was traditional; that the authorship of the Bavli simply received and arranged teachings out of the remote past and did not impart to them a systematic and structured quality. This account of the Bavli as the increment of a sedimentary process, which, by its nature, cannot have been systematic be-

cause it was adventitious, is wrong, and the characterization of the
Bavli as simply a composite of traditions, not a sustained argument, is
uncomprehending. Quite to the contrary, the Bavli in its very nature is
a systematic, and therefore a philosophical document. The two logics,
as well as the sustained representation of dialectic in the abstracts reviewed in Chapters Five and Six, have already alerted us to the philosophical cast of mind of both Talmuds, especially the Bavli. Any
claim that the mind made by the Bavli could not do science because
speculative thinking of a philosophical order, unrestricted as to permitted conclusions and acceptable topics of speculation, was prevented by traditional thinking of an unsystematic character, incapable
of either pursuing curiosity or generalizing, contradicts the character
of the Bavli itself. My proposed reason for the essentially unphiloso-
phical, therefore also unscientific, mind of Judaism will not be
grasped, so long as people dismiss as merely traditional and subser-
vient the intellect that the Judaism of the dual Torah did create.

In fact, the mind of Judaism as the Bavli defined it was not
traditional at all. In the sense that "traditional" teachings derive from
a long process of a sedimentary order, accumulation and conglomeration, tradition is incompatible with the notion of system, and the
Bavli states its ideas whole, complete, and systemically. Let me spell
this out.

"Tradition" may refer to "truth [thought] received," hence to the way
in which revealed truth is transmitted. The word also may speak of
"thought in process of formation," truth that results from a spell of
agglutination and long-term sedimentary formation. Now it is the simple fact that, on its own, a system cannot be traditional in the sense of
coming into being through a sedimentary process, for such a process
by definition develops every which way, not from whole to parts, as in
a systemic composition, but from parts to whole. A system can, and,
in the case of Judaism, always is, traditional in that other sense: truth
revealed and faithfully nurtured and handed on. That is to say, a system may lay claim to the status of traditionality when its framers say
that what they teach derives from a remote past, revelation at Sinai for
example, transmitted faithfully from that point onward.

When people speak of "tradition," they refer to the formative history of a piece of writing, specifically, an incremental and linear process that step by step transmits out of the past an essential and unchanging fundament of truth preserved in writing, by stages, with what one generation has contributed covered by the increment of the next in a sedimentary process, producing a literature that, because of its traditional history as the outcome of a linear and stage by stage process, exercises authority over future generations and therefore is nurtured for the future. In that sense, tradition is supposed to describe a process or a chain of transmission of received materials, refined and corrected but handed on not only unimpaired, but essentially intact. The opening sentence of tractate Abot, "Moses received Torah from Sinai and handed it on to Joshua," bears the implication of such a literary process, though, self-evidently, the remainder of that chapter hardly illustrates the type of process alleged at the outset. The second meaning of tradition bears not upon process but upon content and structure. People sometimes use the word tradition to mean a fixed and unchanging essence deriving from an indeterminate past, a truth bearing its own stigmata of authority, e.g., from God at Sinai. In that sense, of course, the Bavli is traditional — but only in that sense, which is theological, not intellectual.

The reason is that where a cogent statement forms the object of discourse, syllogistic argument and the syntax of sustained thought dominate, obliterating the marks of a sedimentary order of formation in favor of the single and final, systematic one. So far as an authorship proposes to present an account of a system, it will pay slight attention to preserving the indicators of the origins of the detritus of historical tradition, of which, as a matter of fact, the systemic statement itself may well be composed. The threads of the tapestry serve the artist's vision; the artist does not weave so that the threads show up one by one. The weavers make ample use of available yarn. But they weave their own tapestry of thought. And it is their vision and not the character of the threads in hand that dictate the proportions and message of the tapestry. In that same way, so far as processes of thought of a sustained and rigorous character yield writing that makes a single, cogent statement, tradition and system cannot form a compatible unit. Where in the formation of a systemic statement reason governs, it reigns supreme and alone, revising the received materials and, through its own powerful and rigorous logic, restating into a compelling statement the entirety of the prior heritage of information and thought The authorship of the Bavli does not take over, rework, and repeat what it has received out of prior writings but makes its own statement, on its own program, in its own terms, and for its own purposes. And, by the way, it does whatever it wishes with whatever it has received out of the past.

The Bavli, viewed whole and at the end, therefore is not a traditional document. The reason is that, like the Mishnah, the Bavli is formed whole and its authorship has picked and chosen, then arranged for its purposes, each of the parts. The Bavli's statement is one that at each points presents its ideas as a system, whole, complete, ordered and properly balanced. So far as a document is traditional in that, in origin and in composition, it is agglutinative, the Bavli is not a traditional document but one deriving from that sort of systematic and orderly thinking that we associate with the philosophical mind: the work of sustained and thoughtful construction. That statement that the Bavli as a whole makes, specifically, bears many traits that point to cogent and systematic thought — system-building — but few literary or historical traits of that long-term agglutination and conglomeration, such as a sedimentary process yields. In so framing matters, I contrast thought received as truth transmitted through a process of tradition against thought derived from active rationality. And so far as the Bavli exhibits traits of intellect, these are of the same order of rationality and critical acumen as those of any other product of philosophical thinking.

Nothing out of the past can be shown to have dictated the Bavli's program, which is essentially the work of its authorship. But the program, as to logics, of the Bavli's authorship so shaped the mind of Judaism as to yield one kind of thought rather than another. That authorship took command of the whole of the received Torah, both oral, the Mishnah, and written, Scripture. Their remarkable contribution was to turn both documents into sources for the connection of fixed association that defined the Bavli's principle logic of composition, namely, cogency among and between intermediate and the largest units of thought. The organizers and redactors of the materials compiled in the Bavli did something unprecedented within the received canonical writings prior to the formation of the Bavli itself. They allowed sustained passages of Scripture to serve as main beams in the composition of structure and order, as much as sustained, and not merely episodic, passages of the Mishnah served for that purpose. The authorship of the Tosefta and the Yerushalmi had appealed for structure and composition only (Tosefta) or principally (Yerushalmi) to the Mishnah.

By contrast, in a single document, the Bavli's authorship determined, the Mishnah and Scripture would function together and for the first time in much the same way as the (nearly) co-equal sources of fixed associations. Accordingly, both Scripture and the Mishnah now served as source for fixed associations of sustaining dimensions. In the Bavli the Scripture serves alongside the Mishnah and in volume large-scale compositions resting on sequential verses of Scripture or scriptural themes form nearly as large a proportion of the whole as do equivalent compositions built upon Mishnah-exegesis. It follows that both Scripture and the Mishnah in the Bavli together define structure and impart proportion and organization and therefore serve as sources for a repertoire of fixed associations. It is no accident that authentic avatars of the classical literature of Judaism even today learn Scripture through the Bavli's citations of verses of Scripture just as much as, commonly, they learn the Mishnah and assuredly interpret it exactly as the Bavli presents it.

Knowing that fact, we turn to the question of why the mind made by the Bavli failed to pursue philosophy, including natural philosophy, and why, to the present day, do we find in the world of the Judaism of the dual Torah appeal to connections deriving from the revealed Torah but not from nature?

There would ultimately be no science in the mind of Judaism because the remarkable trait of mind of the Bavli's authorship was its emphasis, for large-scale constructive thought, upon the logic of fixed association. That emphasis derived from our authorship's seeing as sources of fixed association not only the Mishnah but also Scripture. And that fact leads us to identify fixed association in a new mode as our authorship's main trait of mind in the construction of the great compositions of knowledge and of thought. Not only so, but that logic of fixed association would dictate yet another strength of the Bavli, namely, its exposition of the linkages of thought, the processes of argument, and not merely the consequences of thought, the upshot and proposition of discourse alone. Let me state matters with heavy emphasis:

These two — [1] fixed association as the principal constructive logic for large-scale composition, [2] exposure of the processes of thought in dialectical argument focused on details or ad hoc issues -- formed the sources of the very strength of the document. But the Bavli's authorship's stunning redefinition of the sources of fixed association, its compositors' compelling exposition of the linkages and connections of argument through an on-going statement of the movement of thought we call dialectical argument — these two indicative traits of intellect dictated, also, the limitations, as to philosophy and natural science, that the heirs of the document would exhibit.

In so stating, I have moved far ahead of my argument. I now turn back and take the steps one by one. The authorship of the Bavli constructed the document that formed the centerpiece of the Judaism of the dual Torah from the seventh century onward. Access to the Torah, written and oral, both Scripture and the Mishnah for the Judaism of the dual Torah that predominated commenced in the pages of the Bavli. The Bavli defined the curriculum of Judaism in its schooling of all males from birth to death. Study of the Torah formed the principal religious activity, and when people studied the Torah, what they learned, in particular, is what they found when they opened the pages of the Bavli. True, other writing went forward; the Bavli hardly marked the end of the intellectual activity of the Judaism of the dual Torah. But the Bavli defined the royal road, the point of departure of all thought, the text demanding commentary and response, the source of truth to which all other truths accommodated themselves, from which all other nourishing truths flowed. That representation of the Bavli as the culturally definitive statement of the Judaism of the dual Torah sets forth the fact but does not explain it. Why the Bavli imposed upon the mind of Judaism its particular configuration is not explained by the enduring and definitive influence of the Bavli. Why people turned to the Bavli is beside the point; what happened to their intellectual lives because they did forms the center of our interest. What I propose to explain is why the Bavli because of its particular character as a piece of writing exercised remarkable formative power upon the mind of Judaism.

Because of the character of the Bavli as a piece of writing, the modes of thought paramount in the Bavli shaped the mind and imagination of generations to come. For the authorship of the Bavli taught not only what to think, but how to think. The authorship of the Bavli exhibited in public the reasoning behind its results. It would follow that generations nurtured on the study of the Bavli would be educated to find self-evident not only the propositions of the Bavli but also its processes of thought, specifically, of analysis, the making of connections, and of synthesis, the drawing of conclusions. Because the Bavli records an on-going conversation, a dialectic without a final stopping point, the conversation never ended, and later generations could locate for themselves a place within it. And making intelligible statements within the intellectual syntax and structure of the Bavli, age succeeding age carried forward those principles of cogency and argument that found initial definition in the pages of the Bavli itself. That is why process, not only proposition, imposed upon the intellect of succeeding generations that character that the shared mind of Judaism exhibited. And from our perspective, a particular aspect of that dialectic, which the Bavli's ebb and flow of argument conveys, takes on special importance.

The reason — the source of the Bavli's power to shape intellectual life — therefore is that the sustained discourse of the Bavli exposed the processes of reasoning, the making of distinctions, the discerning of connections, the drawing of conclusions, that lay behind decisions of law and theology. Indeed, the bulk of the writing, as we saw in the preceding chapter, is devoted not to the presentation of facts but to the exposition of the connections between them. The reader will already have noticed the difference in discourse between the Yerushalmi and the Bavli and all the other writings we briefly surveyed, the Mishnah, Tosefta, Sifra, Sifré to Numbers, Sifré to Deuteronomy, Leviticus Rabbah, the Fathers and The Fathers According to Rabbi Nathan. The former devote attention not only to propositions but to analysis. The latter present propositions, and, where analysis or methodical argument gets under way, it is either highly formalized, as in Sifra and the two Sifrés, or it is given only implicitly, as in Leviticus Rabbah. The two Talmuds by contrast unpack and expose the interstices of thought, the distinctions, disharmonies, anomalies, as well as the paths to harmonization and regularity, that, all together, constitute the decision-making process. An intellectual world nurtured on the Bavli, in particular, will have found the argument the thing. And the schools of the Judaism of the dual Torah conducted as a principal mode of on-going activity highly ritualized argument. Accordingly, the Bavli's very character as writing insured that its authorship would impose their definition not only upon the propositions of the faith, but also upon the shape of intellect and of mind of Judaism. And that mode of thinking — of making connections and drawing conclusions — would thrive wherever, and for so long as, Jews formed life and community in response to the one whole Torah of Moses, our Rabbi, revealed by God at Sinai, or, in secular language, defined culture by opening the pages of the Bavli.

What is it that makes possible the very distinctive character of the Bavli's discourse? It is its moving, or dialectical, argument, which flows from point to point in an unbroken stream of conversation, is the sense of the connectedness of thought that animates the whole. That is what displays the interstices of argument, the movement of thought, and assures that all may participate in the process of reaching a decision, not merely accept the results of the process, the mere decision. The Bavli is not a source of information, but a model of rightly-conducted inquiry. Even the brief snippets we examined in the

preceding chapters, both of the Yerushalmi and of the Bavli, show
how their authorships have put together discrete sentences in such a
way that the connections between one and the next, or between one
set and the next, are fully exposed in exquisite detail. The connections
are shown to derive not from proposition — "let us prove this, by
appealing to the following facts," in the manner of Aphrahat or the
authorships of the Mishnah, Leviticus Rabbah, the metapropositional
compositions of the two Sifrés, and the like — but from a shared,
prior, and a priori program.

And what lies at the foundation of the dialectical argument? It
is the logic of fixed association. That is to say, the fundamental logic
of the dialectical argument, the principle by which cogency is imputed
to two or more sentences in succession, is that same logic of fixed association that joins the very largest units of thought into a single sustained document, a treatment of a Mishnah-paragraph, a treatise on a
Mishnah-tractate, upward to the Bavli as a whole. True, earlier we noticed how smaller units of discourse, paragraphs in common par-
lance, hung together because of a shared proposition. Yet a second
glance shows us that even here, a sizable component of discrete and
individual sentences finds its place as well. And well it should, when
what links three independent facts or sentences, not of the same classification at all, for instance — in my earlier representation, episodic
statements of the classification A to 3 to # — is simply the movement
itself, this, then that, then the other thing, connected every which way,
and, more than a few times, adventitiously at best. And, given the clear
sense of the compositors that they have, in fact, composed a cogent
document made up of cogent compositions themselves comprising
connected sentences, we have to conclude that dialectical argument
appeals in the end to that logic of fixed association. That is what
makes it necessary to maintain and sustain the movement that defines
dialectical argument.

Moving from one thing to the next, and by the way, there is
this also to consider, but then this leads to that — that characterization of the dialectical argument, such as my repertoire of examples
yields, tells us what holds the whole together. And it is that sense of

the givenness of connection that makes unnecessary the disciplined composition of a sustained and well-constructed argument, proposition, proof, argument, and the like. If we ask the source of the fixed association, it is principally the Mishnah and Scripture -- the oral and written media of the one whole Torah of Moses, our rabbi. But, of course, once "we all know" the relevance of this, that, and the other thing, then fixed association derives from a variety of sources, some of them explicit, others merely a matter of intellectual convention. From the perspective of our inquiry, the source of fixed association — a text, known order or sequence of events, a list of this and that or merely a sense, at the deep structure of mind, that this really does yield that — yields no consequence. What matters in the end is that the association of one thing to the next bears two traits. First, it is fixed, excluding free association. Second, it is imputed or supplied, not discovered or achieved by the engaged participants to discourse. The former trait insures rational discourse, which then is publicly accessible. The latter precludes inquiry into matters beyond the framework of the convention of fixed association (whatever it is), except within the limits of reason defined by that convention. So while scientific argument may move in a dialectical manner, talmudic argument would not yield science.

That is why I have argued that it is the very power of the Bavli, namely, its exposition of its modes of thought and the steps of argument, that also constitutes its pathos, its strength, its weakness. For the two absolutely necessary traits of mind of philosophy, including natural philosophy, require, first, systematically thinking about propositions in a philosophical manner, and, second, highly speculative pursuit of wherever curiosity leads. The mode of thought of the Bavli requires the former but precludes the latter. Dialectical argument, which appeals for connection to extrinsic points of intersection, e.g., with a common third element, may or may not yield philosophical argument about propositions. But a logic of fixed association, which, I have argued, to begin with makes possible the dialectical argument that distinguishes the Bavli, assuredly imposes limits upon the free run of curiosity hither and yon. For fixed association is just that:

fixed, imposed, defined from without. And the very fixedness of association is what makes possible dialectical argument, without the danger of chaos and descent into caprice and irrationality. For a moving argument without a predetermined route and program of progress can descend into mere free association, that is to say, babble legitimated not rationally but merely politically. But fixed association, while necessary for the exposition of the links and stages of the rigorous argument of the Bavli, also is what makes unlikely the free pursuit of curiosity wherever it leads: why this, not that? Once more, power and pathos unite. The strength of dialectic rests upon fixed association, which protects the integrity of discourse. The weakness of dialectic is this same fixed association, limiting, as it does, the potentialities of inquiry to a pre-assigned program and predetermined limits.

True, when we ask whether the Bavli's authorship has defined a mode of thought that would facilitate, or discourage, propositional discourse, we answer in the affirmative. The interior obstacle to philosophical inquiry is not set by the Bavli's basic mode of thought, which is indeed propositional. In Chapter Five we noted the sophisticated character of metapropositional discourse and found its best exemplification in the pages of the Yerushalmi and — this only by implication — the Bavli as well, for the authorships of both documents pursue a narrowly-methodical mode of analysis of the Mishnah; we can always predict what questions will be addressed to any discrete passage; and we therefore prove the presence, within the discrete facts of the document, of rules, regularities, principles of order -- a profoundly scientific inquiry. Not only so, but the other intermediate units of discourse and thought (paragraphs, in common language) that we reviewed in both chapters invariably demonstrate a strong interest in sustained and cogent, philosophical discourse, the mounting of arguments, the drawing of conclusions.

As to the power of the Bavli's mode of thought, at the intermediate level, to stimulate speculative curiosity, I need only point to the systematic pursuit of fresh questions characteristic of the sample in our hand in Chapter Six. That seems to me to exemplify a mode of thought fully able to do more than merely stimulate the rehearsal and classification of received information, the sifting and refining of tradition. It is a mode of thought that also, and especially, provokes and precipitates free and wide-ranging speculation on hitherto-unimagined possibilities. The Bavli's authorship inaugurated an on-going tradition of thought, in which later generations found for themselves a distinctive position. Commentaries pursuing issues not suggested within the Bavli itself, codes of law organizing the result of thought in entirely fresh ways, decisions on questions wholly outside of the program of the original document — all three modes of fresh speculation testify to the potentialities of the Bavli to precipitate and generate speculation of a systematic and also a propositional order. So at the center of matters is not the issue of propositional thought, of which the Bavli presents an ample and sophisticated example. It is the manner of making connections and — consequently, inexorably and unavoidably — also the drawing of conclusions, that is, that very centerpiece of mind that I identified at the outset as characteristic of the writings of the Judaism of the dual Torah. The mode of argument, and not the character of the propositions, is what made unlikely the development of science as part of the philosophical tradition.

Since the authorship of the Bavli set the example of writing in a highly speculative manner and scarcely engaged in the mere rehashing of tradition, it follows that heirs to their mode of thought, properly trained, also would think in ways that were highly speculative, not simply rehashing "tradition." But the authorship of the Bavli, while exhibiting attitudes of speculative and propositional character entirely congruent with those of philosophy, were not philosophers in large scale processes of overall procedure. The reason, to review, is simple. They joined facts in a way different from the philosophical, and they drew conclusions from facts in a way different from that of philosophy. Once connections came from without, the making of connections and drawing of conclusions would derive from that same received program of inquiry.

The received program of fixed associations hardly stimulated looking to the world beyond the Torah, whether the world of nature or the world of social history. It is not because people within the

Bavli's intellectual framework avoided making generalizations or presenting conclusions in an orderly and systematic way. That is beside the point, and it also is not true. It is because people used to receiving associations within a fixed and available program found slight stimulus to observe associations on their own, to ask their "why this, not that" in circumstances in which "this" and "that" join together not in fixed and available intersection but solely in the mind of an observer. Nature and social history did not form realms in which people would anticipate associating facts and explaining the association by drawing conclusion. The received program of the Torah, written and oral, set forth those realms in which people would expect to associate two unrelated facts and explain their intersection, unity, difference or harmony. I underline that nothing in the topicality of nature or the history of nations set those subjects beyond the pale; the reason that the heirs of the Bavli did not pursue natural philosophy or social philosophy — we should today call the one natural science, the other social science or (more narrowly) history — is not that the Bavli ruled out as inconsequential those vast areas of knowledge. It is — to repeat — because those areas of learning contained within themselves no program of fixed association, except as they found their way into the pages of the Torah, written and oral, set forth in the Bavli. Creation, the history of humanity — natural and social science — found ample consideration in those pages, but solely through points of intersection and association imputed, wholly extrinsically and from without, by the adventitious character of the Torah, oral and written, set forth by the Bavli. And, in the nature of things, on that basis there could be no science, whether natural or social. To state matters very simply, the Mishnah, with its propositional and syllogistic argument concern the nature of things, can have generated natural and social science; the Bavli could not and did not.

And that is why they produced philosophy only by abandoning the Bavli, and also why those who did not abandon the Bavli produced no philosophy, or, therefore, science. It was the Bavli's *and*, and not the *equal*, that formed the insuperable obstacle to science. The mode of propositional thought of a philosophical character, the equal, worked well, the mode of putting two and two together, the and did not, for the formation of science. Let me state matters simply: why in the mind of the Judaism of the dual Torah was there no science in particular, even when there could be philosophy? Because in a system of fixed texts, you need a fixed text to make connection, and nature provides no fixed texts.

Let me state the next step in my proposition with equally heavy emphasis: *In forming the large world in which everything would be contained in some one thing, the Bavli's authorship relied for connection upon the received text, and necessarily drew conclusions resting upon connection solely within the dictates of an a priori and imputed system of making connections. These connections supplied and not discovered, structures ultimately imputed through extrinsic processes of thought, not nurtured through the proposal and testing of propositions intrinsic to the matter at hand.*

In the rather odd language I introduced on earlier pages, in the mind of Judaism you have an *and* and you have *an equal* or a therefore, but you do not have both an and and an equal or a therefore. The *and* comes from an extrinsic source, a source not deriving from connections we see among facts we think congruent or even interesting, and any equal or therefore that we then propose will not attend to the propositions implicit in the facts (whether those of nature, leading to natural philosophy or natural science, or those of history, leading to social philosophy or social science).

At issue then is not the topics defined as important by the received writing, either Scripture or the Mishnah. Science found no interest not because it dealt with subject-matter found trivial, since, after all, Scripture begins with the creation of the world, and in the Mishnah, issues of natural science, physics as then practiced, as well as psychology, for example, do occupy a place of importance. Philosophy, including natural philosophy, began in the making of connections, in asking, why this and also that? The answers, the conclusions drawn, proved adventitious and merely interesting; the making of connections between and among facts is what precipitated the processes of intellect that, by the way, yielded answers. But for the authorship of the Bavli, large structures, encompassing connections among many things — these to begin with derived from without, from the received documents, which joined this to that and so precipitated inquiry into connections between this and that supplied, ultimately and exhaustively, for thought at the largest scale of intellect, by the Torah.

The mode of thought that yielded connections of this kind — connections I have characterized as those imposed through fixed association — made no room for a mode of thought that required the mind itself to discover its own points of intersection or confluence and then — but only then — to ask why. Connection supplied left no space, so it appears, for connection discovered. True, in the Bavli we find both the making of connections and the drawing of conclusions. But in the logic of fixed association that holds the whole together, the connections are provided by fixed associations, and — so it follows — the equal or the therefore does not emerge from same sort of logical thinking that formed the foundation of the fixed association. The equal or the therefore derives from rigorous thinking, the making of distinctions, the search for regularity and order and rule. But to fixed association, proposition, regularity order and rule — these are simply not pertinent. Fixed association puts things together in one way, propositional connection in a different way, and the Bavli's authorship mixed two essentially distinct logic, the one at the intermediate, the other at the fundamental, level of the construction of thought. Thinking philosophically about connections formed non-propositionally, therefore framed in an other-than-philosophical way, in the end produced thought that took for granted the very thing that philosophy, and especially natural philosophy, found at the center of interest, the subject of the most intense curiosity: the connection, why this and that?

Now this characterization of the paramount mode of effecting connection and explaining it contradicts a simple fact, as I have many times hinted. The Judaism of the dual Torah from the advent of Islam did produce an on-going and vital philosophical movement. That movement confronted the philosophical tradition mediated by Islam from antiquity and not only confronted philosophic concepts and norms but also accommodated the received Judaism, in its intellectual framework, to those norms. A Judaic component of philosophy of religion investigated in Judaic terms "issues common to Judaism, Christianity, and Islam, dealing with propositions concerning the existence of god, divine attributes, the creation of the world, the phenomenon of prophecy, the human soul, and general principles of human conduct." That Judaic component of the public philosophy of religion appealed to the canonical writings of the Judaism of the dual Torah.

The medieval philosophical movement appealed not only to Scripture but also to the Rabbinic writings, beginning with the Bavli. Any allegation such as I have made that the modes of thought of the Bavli posed obstacles to philosophical thinking in general, and inquiry into natural philosophy in particular, has to address that fact. Since anyone who knows the history of Jews' intellectual life therefore will quite properly object that there was a philosophical movement in the Judaism of the dual Torah, and one of considerable consequence, two simple considerations deserve attention.

First, all Judaic philosophers, while appealing to the canonical writings, also formed their intellectual programs and methods in response to the philosophical writings of ancient Greece, mediated through Islam. Accordingly, the formation of a Judaic philosophical tradition derived not from the Judaism of the dual Torah and its mode of thought but from another source and in accord with a different mode of thought from that of the canonical literature.

Second, the philosophical tradition enjoyed only limited influence. Where education and the definition of the Torah encompassed only the Bavli and related writings, the philosophical tradition was excluded. Only where intellectuals mastered a second, and separate intellectual tradition did the modes of thought of philosophy, including science, make an important impact. That fact once again underlines my simple assertion that distinctive modes of thought derived from distinct sources of learning, and that the mind of the Judaism of the dual Torah as defined by the Bavli proved ultimately not propositional and assuredly not philosophical. Institutions devoted to the study of the Bavli and related writings proliferated; the community of Judaism turned to the Bavli for guidance in the conduct of public business and private life. The schools and public bodies devoted to the Bavli vastly outweighed in influence the philosophical movement. That movement was made up of individuals, who read one another's books and wrote for one another; few philosophers defined public discourse or greatly shaped the shared intellectual life of the community of Israel. Among the philosophers within Judaism issues of philosophy and science did enjoy ample attention; but the Judaism of the dual Torah even in their time went its own way, essentially unchanged by the philosophical movement and its propositional logic of discourse. So the exception proves the rule: the Judaism of the dual Torah defined discourse as the Bavli taught it to, and that discourse in the aggregate of the world of Judaism made slight provision for philosophy, including natural philosophy. The correlation between the presence of the philosophical mode of thought and exposure to philosophy, in addition to talmudic study, strongly sustains the proposition at hand.

Not only so, but, it is also generally conceded, philosophical modes of thought appeared new and threatening, so Baron: "...The first to come to grips with these new problems were the heterodox members of each community."[2] But the masters of the Bavli and its associated writings were the opposite of heterodox. They rightly claimed to define what was orthodox. The impetus for philosophy came out of the initial encounter with Aristotle, and there too, the sense that that represented something external and demanded harmonization with a mode of thinking, as well as specific beliefs, differ-

---

[2] A comprehensive and accessible account is provided by Salo Wittmayer Baron, *A Social and Religious History of the Jews* (Philadelphia, 1958: The Jewish Publication Society of America). Second edition, revised and enlarged. *High Middle Ages. 500-1200: Volumes III-VIII. VIII. Philosophy and Science, pp. 55-138. For science, including medicine, pp. 138-268.* All allegations as to fact in what follows derive from Baron

ent from the Aristotelian, is explicit in all accounts of philosophy. It hardly requires rehearsal of the established facts of the philosophical movement in Judaism, therefore, to point to those facts as ample support for my thesis on the making of the mind of Judaism. From the Bavli forward, it would be a mode of intellectual life in which appeal for cogency — connection, explanation of connection — would prove dual: propositional at the near-horizon, fixed associative at the largest scale of thought.

A second important objection to my account of why the mind of Judaism did not encompass science in particular is that, of course, it did. Within the rich philosophical tradition of Judaism in medieval times flourished a scientific and medical one, so Baron: "With the same passionate faith in the power of reason that characterized their quest for metaphysical and theological certainty, the Jewish thinkers under Islam began coping with the expanding horizons of scientific knowledge." Baron points to the impetus for scientific thinking and even research. It did not derive from the Bavli or any other document of the inherited Torah. It derived from knowledge of Greek science and Roman science: Euclid, Ptolemy, Galen, for example. Not only so, but conflict between doctrines as to facts of the natural world deriving from science and observation and those implicit in the Torah, encompassing the oral Torah, testifies to the simple claim I have made. The impetus for scientific work, the modes of pursuing it both in intellect and in observation and even experiment — these came from sources of thought other than the talmudic, and they also appealed for self-evidence in observation and explanation — making connections, drawing conclusions — to a mind other than the Bavli's. It is one thing to allege that medieval scientists who were Jews characteristically cited biblical or Rabbinic proof-texts for scientific propositions or proposed to harmonize their results with the Torah, oral or written. It is another to maintain that the modes of thought guiding scientific work accord with the modes of thought imbued by talmudic learning. Here too, the impetus and the method came from elsewhere. That mathematics was held to waste time better spent in Torah-study is only one obvious piece of evidence pointing toward the simple conclusion I have drawn. The simple fact is that the Bavli and associated writings defined both what was worth knowing and what knowing required; the claim was exclusive and those who thought otherwise, in both philosophy in general and natural philosophy in particular, found need to justify and validate doing the work they did, not to mention holding the conclusions that they reached.

To conclude: the mind of Judaism appealed to four logics in its quest for what linked one thing to another. Three of these logics — the propositional, the metapropositional, and the teleological — are entirely commonplace for the West, and the fourth — the fixed associative — can be understood as well. All four carried forward that same program of thinking that we in the West have always understood to be the address and task of philosophy and today quite reasonably identify with science. It is the effort to put two and two together and therefore to explain four, or, stated more abstractly, to find, in the language of Robin Horton cited earlier, "unity underlying apparent diversity...simplicity underlying apparent complexity,...order underlying apparent disorder...regularity underlying apparent anomaly." I identify two discrete facts (my "two" and "two") with diversity, complexity, disorder, anomaly, and the making of connection between them (my "and" and "equal") as the quest for unity, simplicity, order, and regularity. The proposition yielded by the making of connection, the drawing of conclusions or the offering of hypotheses — these form the counterpart to the modes of thought, whether of tradition or of science, that contemporary classifications of thought identify. We recognize that the distinctive union of two modes of thought, the propositional and the fixed associative, trained the mind of Judaism to find unity, simplicity, order, regularity — in all, self-evident explanation — in a distinctive way. That way served to draw together tradition and system, to allow systematic thought to generate propositions, and also to present those propositions in such a way as to affirm and validate the received Torah of Sinai, written and oral. Systematic thought arranged as if it came from revelation constituted the mode of discourse that Judaism defined, and that served exceedingly well for a very long time.

If I had to offer a single reason for the subordination of philosophy and proposition, paramount in the Bavli's intermediate discourse, to the principle of large-scale organization defined by received associations, predominant in the Bavli's large compositions of orderly thought, I should point to the happy outcome. The effect of organizing large-scale discourse in one way, intermediate in the other, is to present the result of (philosophical, propositional) thought in such a way as to underline continuity, back to Sinai, of all such thought. The system as a whole is therefore so constituted as to preserve freedom in the framework of continuity, change in the setting of tradition, and to do so by stating the legitimation of the whole at the most profound levels of the life of intellect. In this setting, therefore, we find a correspondence between modes of thought in the life of intellect and the politics of the community of the Judaism of the dual Torah. The rules of the one conformed to the theological apologetic necessary for the other, the free and vigorous working of the one validated the social sanctions necessary to sustain the other. Modes of thought and the mores of the social world, the ethics of the mind and the ethos of the mediating world beyond -- these attained that remarkable correspondence that imparted to the whole a self-evidence that was at one and the same time intellectual and concrete. And that is why the system worked. In context, not producing philosophy, including science, hardly imposed too high a price to pay.

Linking what you and I think to the (putative) exegesis of the Mishnah or Scripture secures for us all a place in the chain of tradition to Moses, our rabbi, on Sinai. Doing so a moreover succeeds in securing for mind itself that speculative freedom to explore and test propositions that thought requires. When I argued, earlier in this chapter, that the Bavli was systematic and therefore not traditional, I set aside the form of the document in favor of an account of its structure and inner cogency of mind. But the form does create a powerful effect and did define thought not only thought but the apologetic for thought. The form — connections imputed, but conclusions declared only in the context of received writings — imparted its imprint upon intellect as well. The balance, order, proportion, sense of composition of the whole — these definitive traits of the mind of Judaism worked exceedingly well, so long as they worked, in holding together the two requirements of mind: freedom to speculate, responsibility to compose and construct for age succeeding age — therefore (in the mythic framework) from eternity to the end of time.

But philosophy and therefore also natural philosophy demanded what the mind of the Judaism of the dual Torah could not — and can never — concede. And that was the datum that the quest for unity in diversity, simplicity in complexity, order in disorder, and regularity in anomaly, engaged only humanity's mind, but not God's too. All Judaisms, including especially the normative one of the dual Torah, knew to search for unity, simplicity, order, regularity, and therefore explanation, because to begin with God created the world as unified, simple, orderly, regular, and therefore subject and susceptible to explanation. The premise that one might go in quest for systematic knowledge derived for the Judaism of the dual Torah from the Torah, which recorded, for humanity to know, God's work in making the world and in forming Israel for the sanctification of the here and now and the salvation of the world at the end of time. Philosophy began with not knowledge but search for knowledge, and the mind of Judaism began with a quest made possible, to begin with, by the character of the human mind, made, as it was, "in our image, after our likeness."

Judaism therefore could not, on its own, generate philosophy, not because issues of a propositional character intervened, or even because modes of thought vastly differed, but because philosophy ended where Judaism began. The Judaism of the dual Torah could not deny the knowledge that to begin with the mind of Judaism encompassed. The upshot is simple. What philosophy sought — unity, simplicity, order, regularity — is that very destination at which the quest of the mind of the Judaism of the dual Torah commenced. What the one wanted the other knew it had. And in consequence what the mind of that Judaism was meant to make possible was therefore a different search altogether from the philosophical and the scientific, which was, and is, that search for God whose being formed the unity, the simplicity, the order, the regularity, to which, in the mythic language of faith, sanctification in the world and salvation at the end of time referred.

For sanctification spoke of all things bearing each its rightful name, the correct ordering of all reality in the natural world, and salvation addressed the right and true ordering, thus ending of all reality in the world of society, therefore of history. The one can have yielded scientific proposition, the other teleological proposition, and, in the context of the Torah, each did. But the mind of Judaism accomplished its tasks in its way, using its language, in response to the logics self-evident in its circumstance and perception of the world. For the task of a quest for the explanation of how things intersected and made sense drew the mind of Judaism into the Torah, record of God's plan and program for the world, And that has made all the difference. And, if I may conclude as a believing Jew, it still can — it still can.